MYTHS AND MYSTERIES

OF

TENNESSEE

MYTHS AND MYSTERIES

OF
TENNESSEE

TRUE STORIES
OF THE UNSOLVED AND UNEXPLAINED

SUSAN SAWYER

gpp

Guilford, Connecticut

Copyright © 2013 by Morris Book Publishing, LLC

Map by Alena Joy Pearce © Morris Book Publishing, LLC
Project Editor: Lynn Zelem
Layout: Lisa Reneson

Library of Congress Cataloging-in-Publication Data is available on file.

ISBN 978-0-7627-7230-8

Printed in the United States of America
10 9 8 7 6 5 4 3 2 1

CONTENTS

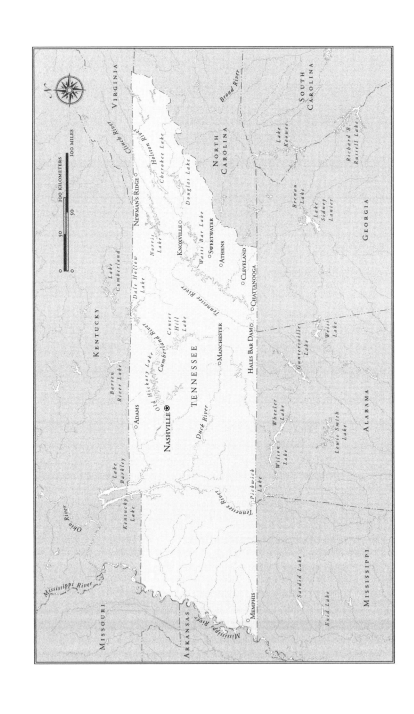

INTRODUCTION

As a sixth-generation Tennessean, I love learning about and sharing intriguing stories from my home state. In *Myths and Mysteries of Tennessee,* you'll find fourteen fascinating tales associated with the Volunteer State, ranging from sightings of ghostly spirits to accounts of legendary characters.

People often ask, "What's your favorite story about Tennessee?" In the case of *Myths and Mysteries of Tennessee,* the answer is easy for me. The story about "The Haunted Hales Bar Dam" holds a special place in my heart. My grandfather, Alvin Spears, served as the lockmaster for Hales Bar Lock and Dam during the 1920s. My father and his two sisters were among the many children who trudged through the spooky tunnel beneath the Tennessee River as they went back and forth from school and home. I grew up hearing lots of stories about the leaky old tunnel, which paranormal investigators now say holds supernatural energy . . . or maybe the curse of a Cherokee chief. Once you read the chapter, it's up to you to decide!

From the legendary Davy Crockett to a mystery mummy in Memphis, these captivating stories take us to a time and place that most of us have never experienced. Please enjoy the journey as you read about some of the most unusual and fantastic tales of Tennessee's history and culture. And please visit my wonderful home state and uncover a mystery or two of your own!

Susan Sawyer
Chattanooga, Tennessee

CHAPTER 1

The Bell Witch Haunting

Life was good for the John Bell family in 1816. Since moving from North Carolina to northern Robertson County, Tennessee, in 1804, John and Lucy Bell had made their home on more than three hundred acres of farmland in the Red River Settlement, north of Nashville. As they raised their seven children and farmed the rich, fertile land, the Bells prospered and became well-respected members of the community.

From 1817 to 1821, however, a strange series of events shattered the Bell's peaceful life in rural Tennessee. These mysterious events would become known as one of America's best-known ghost stories.

The first strange incident happened while John was inspecting his corn field. Encountering a creature with the head of a rabbit and the body of a dog, John aimed his rifle at the animal. After he fired several shots, the creature vanished. Later that evening, mysterious noises reverberated throughout the Bell's log home, sounding as though someone—or something—was knocking against the exterior shutters and the back door. As the mysterious beating sounds continued, night after night, throughout the fall and winter, John would leap to the door, determined to catch the culprit. But as soon as he reached the door, the noises would stop.

By spring the family heard more unexplainable sounds inside the house—rats gnawing on bed posts in the two bedrooms of the Bell sons, Richard, Joel, John Jr., and Drewry. Each time one of the brothers would open the door to investigate, the noises suddenly stopped. By daylight no one could find any evidence of rats.

Gradually the antics of the invisible creature grew bolder. The bedcovers of the children slowly slipped off their beds, and the family heard noises that sounded as though someone was smacking his lips, choking, or strangling. Then it sounded as though stones were smashing against the roof, animals were fighting outside, and chains were being dragged across the floors.

By 1818 the bed coverings were no longer being slowly slipped away from the children as they slept. Instead, the blankets and sheets were being furiously stripped and yanked away. But the final proof that something supernatural had invaded the Bell home came when the force awakened the Bells' daughter, Betsy, by yanking on her hair and dragging her out of bed. Even more frightening was the realization that the force attacked Richard, Betsy's brother, at the same time. Apparently, the thing possessed the ability to attack two people simultaneously in separate rooms.

Baffled, John and his wife knew they had to confide in someone about the increasingly disturbing phenomena in their home. Active members of the Red River Baptist Church, the Bells invited their fellow church members and closest neighbors, James and Rebecca Johnston, to spend the night in their home. A religious man, James read Scripture to the Bell family, and the group joined hands, prayed, and asked the Lord to cast away the demons invading the Bell home.

The Johnstons then retired to one of the upstairs bedrooms. With all the candles extinguished throughout the house, the spirit arrived with full force with the noises of rats gnawing on bedposts, stones hurling down on the roof, and covers ripping from the beds. Each time James rose to light a candle, the noises would move to another room. Eventually the spirit stopped in Betsy's room and yanked on her hair. Just as the Johnstons burst into the room, candles lighting their way, the sharp sound of a hand smacking flesh echoed through the room. Betsy's face snapped to the side from the force of the blow at least six more times before the spirit began dragging her around the room by her hair. When James ordered the spirit to stop, Betsy's head hit the floor as the force let go of her hair.

James convinced John Bell that he and his family could not continue to endure this any longer on their own. The next day, as the Red River community was informed of the months of torture the Bell family had experienced, neighbors and fellow church members tried to offer explanations for the mysterious events.

Elizabeth "Betsy" Bell, 1894, from *An Authenticated History of the Famous Bell Witch: The Wonder of the 19th Century, and Unexplained Phenomenon of the Christian Era* by M. V. Ingram.

Were minor earthquakes erupting beneath the Bells' home, causing the noises and tremors? Was Betsy perpetrating a hoax?

The church pastor, Rev. Sugg Fort, suggested that a meddlesome neighbor, Kate Batts, was somehow responsible for the strange happenings. After years of observing Kate's odd behavior, some residents of the Red River community labeled the outspoken, forceful Kate as a witch. Moreover, a land dispute between the Bells and the Battses had prompted Kate to file suit against John Bell in court. The Robertson County Circuit Court ruled in favor of Kate, and a jury convicted John. During a public confrontation John accused Kate of being a "lying witch." John's fellow elders at Red River Baptist Church felt that they had no choice but to expel him from the church for his accusation. Kate warned John that sad changes would soon descend upon him and his family, and openly cast a curse upon the Bells.

To test the spirit, visitors to the Bell home would ask questions. How many rooms were in the house? How many people were in the room? The spirit would respond with the appropriate number of knocks on the walls or clawing on the floors.

The creature took another dimension in 1819 as it began to whisper to family members and visitors who tried to converse with it. When John Jr. asked the spirit to identify itself, the whispered feminine voice revealed that it had once been a living person.

Betsy remained the primary focus of the spirit's physical abuse. A lovely young girl, she attracted the attention of Joshua Gardner, a handsome young man in the community. Once the spirit warned Betsy not to marry Joshua, however, Betsy promptly broke the engagement.

Word of the Bell witch spread well beyond the borders of Robertson County. Over the next few years, visitor after visitor paraded through the Bell home in hopes of taming the spirits that lived there. All left soon after they arrived, admitting defeat at the invisible hands of the smart-mouthed spirit.

According to local legend, one of the visitors to the Bell home was Gen. Andrew Jackson. About a mile before reaching the Bell home, the wagon carrying supplies for Jackson and his entourage suddenly stopped. Though four strong, capable horses were pulling the wagon across dry, flat land, the wagon would not move. General Jackson dismounted his horse, and he and his men pushed the wagon from front to back and from side to side. But the wagon could not be budged.

Baffled, Jackson laughed. "What else can it be but the Bells' witch?" Once Jackson acknowledged the spirit's presence, the wagon easily moved down the road.

Among the men in Jackson's group was a gentleman from Nashville who had a reputation for defeating the supernatural. In the Bell home that evening, the man fully challenged the Bell witch to make her presence known.

The group heard the sound of approaching footsteps, then the voice of the Bell witch, announcing her arrival. She then challenged him to shoot her. The man raised his pistol, but it failed to fire. The Bell witch seized the moment to slap the man to the floor, then picked him up by his nostrils and hurled him out the door.

General Jackson reportedly laughed so hard that he fell to one knee and vowed he would rather face the entire British army than the Bell witch.

At this point the spirit that had invaded their home was taking its toll on the Bell family. John was constantly being attacked by the witch, and Lucy was becoming frail from worry and despair. The witch declared that she would not let up on John until he was dead and buried.

By the fall of 1820, the witch had diverted all of her abuse from Betsy and her siblings directly to John. Facial twitches and swellings plagued the man for days at a time, sometimes accompanied by a swollen tongue that left his speech garbled. In December of that same year, John's twitching intensified, his appetite vanished, and he became too weak to leave his bed. The spirit predicted that John would not live to see the new year.

On the morning of December 19, 1820, John's pulse was so faint that Lucy could barely locate it. John Jr., who usually dispensed his father's medications, found an unfamiliar small bottle located in front of his father's other medicine. When the doctor arrived to check on John, he confirmed that the bottle was not one of the medications that he had brought to the house on previous visits. After checking John the physician confirmed that John would not likely emerge from his coma. He also sniffed the bottle and stated that it smelled very much like the odor from John's mouth. He suspected that the liquid was the juice of poisonous berries.

John's sons retrieved a black cat from the barn and forced it to swallow some of the liquid to see if it was poisonous. Within the hour, they had their answer. The cat fell into a stupor and died.

James Johnston, who had been tending to John at his bedside, reported that the Bell witch had announced that she had brought a vial of poison and given it to John as he slept—and he had taken enough to kill him.

Early the next morning John Bell breathed his last breath. It was reported that the Bell witch even attended the funeral, singing in a drunken stupor. After the funeral the Bell witch spoke to John Jr., promising to soon bid good-bye to the house.

With the absence of the Bell witch, young Betsy blossomed into a beautiful fifteen-year-old and resumed her courtship with handsome Joshua Gardner. The young couple announced their engagement on the Monday after Easter and celebrated with a picnic on the banks of the Red River with several other young couples.

Unable to resist casting his line into the Red River, Joshua Gardner felt a strong tug on his fishing line. An enormous fish was at the end of the line, yanking with such force that it jerked the pole into the water and carried the pole and line upstream. A cool breeze suddenly wafted over the river, coming from the direction of the Bell farm. Betsy must have felt goose bumps up and down her spine as the voice of the Bell witch echoed over the water, warning her not to marry Joshua Gardner.

Betsy raced back to the house, Joshua following closely at her heels. But nothing Joshua could say or do could convince Betsy to marry him. It was obvious to the young woman that the spirit had invaded the Bell home for two purposes: to kill her father and to see that she never married Joshua Gardner.

That evening the spirit whispered to Betsy that it would bother the Bell family no more but reserved the right to reappear within several years.

Joshua Gardner left Tennessee, never to return, after Betsy broke their engagement.

Joshua and Betsy's school teacher, Richard Powell, expressed an interest in Betsy. A courtship gradually evolved between the two that would last three years and culminate in their marriage on March 21, 1824.

In the years that followed, Powell's involvement in society and politics required him to relinquish his schoolmaster job to pursue a career in politics. He served as sheriff of Robertson County between 1830 and 1833 and was elected to the Tennessee House of Representatives in 1833, where he represented Robertson County in the Twentieth Tennessee General Assembly. He made a name for himself as a lawmaker of great ability and gained wide popularity throughout the state. Powell had also been a captain in the Tennessee State Militia, a census enumerator, and a justice of the peace.

According to Brent Monahan, author of *The Bell Witch: An American Haunting*, Richard Powell wrote a manuscript about the Bell witch legend, documenting events as an eyewitness.

While many believe the Bell witch haunting is nothing more than a ghostly legend, others contend that census, church, and court records prove that the places and individuals involved in the Bell witch legend were real. One of the earliest accounts, *An Authenticated History of the Famous Bell Witch,* by M. V. Ingram, published in 1894, centers on a manuscript written by one of the Bell sons in 1846. The manuscript, "Our Family Trouble," is believed to be the only eyewitness account of the haunting. The second account, *A Mysterious Spirit: The Bell Witch of Tennessee,* published in 1934, was written by Dr. Charles Bailey Bell, grandson of John Bell.

More than a dozen books have been written about the Bell witch legend, and movies such as *The Bell Witch Haunting* in 2004 and *An American Haunting,* released in 2005, claim to be based on the mysterious events that took place on the Bell farm in the early 1800s.

According to legend the Bell witch takes full credit for killing John Bell. Some believe the admission is the first time that a spirit admitted and was responsible for someone's death. Others point out that the Bell witch haunting falls into the category of a poltergeist haunting—caused by unseen spirits performing supernatural feats, such as moving furniture and slapping people.

Today the John Bell farm is still being used as farmland by private owners. The land once known as the Red River

Settlement was renamed Adams Station in the mid-nineteenth century, and is now known as Adams, Tennessee. The farmhouse is long gone, but one original element from the legend is a cave on the former Bell property. The cave was added to the National Register of Historic Places in 2008, and its current owners operate tours of the site.

CHAPTER 2

The Secrets of the Lost Sea

Growing up in the foothills of the Great Smoky Mountains, Ben Sands loved to explore the caves near his home in Monroe County, Tennessee. But little did the young boy realize he would stumble upon a discovery deep inside the earth that would become known as one of the world's most mysterious and legendary bodies of water.

As a thirteen-year-old boy living near Sweetwater, Tennessee, in 1905, Ben must have heard countless tales about the extensive and historic cave system in the area called Craighead Caverns. The series of large, underground caves, named in honor of Chief Craighead, were occupied by Cherokee Indians long before the first settlers arrived in Tennessee. Indian artifacts ranging from pottery and arrowheads to weapons and jewelry were later discovered in a large room of the cave now known as "the Council Room," nearly a mile from the entrance.

From the tiny natural opening on the side of the mountain, the cave expands into a series of huge rooms. Young Ben often accompanied his father in the caves as he led groups who were hunting for arrowheads. Although locals had heard rumors of a large underground lake somewhere deep within the cave, no one had actually seen a body of water.

One day Ben decided to explore the cave by himself. The adventurous young man wiggled through a small, muddy opening that he had never dared to venture through before, probably not realizing that he was three hundred feet underground. To his astonishment, he discovered the small entrance opened up into a room so enormous that the glow of his lantern could not capture all of the area. Even more remarkable was the fact that the vast, dark cavern was filled with an endless sea of water.

Captivated by both the vastness of the cave and his inability to see the far side of the lake, Ben decided to test the waters, literally. The young boy made balls of mud and hurled them in every direction, hoping one of them would land beyond the body of water on an unseen shore. But time after time Ben heard only splashes of water echoing through the darkness.

Returning home, Ben must have been thrilled to tell of his discovery of an underground sea in the old caverns. To his dismay, however, few people believed him. A lake beneath the earth? *Impossible,* they said. The rumor about a lost sea in Craighead Caverns was nothing more than an old Cherokee legend.

In time Ben convinced his father to return to the cave with him so he could prove to the elder Sands that the lake was not a figment of his imagination. Unfortunately, rising water levels blocked the small opening into the underground lake from Ben and his father, hiding the entrance from them.

Skepticism about Ben's geological find, along with droughts that caused the water levels to fluctuate, lingered for several years until local explorers stumbled upon the underground lake again. And it would be decades before Ben realized that he had discovered the largest underground lake in the United States, the second largest in the world—a four and one-half acre body of water, three hundred feet beneath the earth's surface.

As the years passed, other explorers discovered long-lost secrets about the cave. In 1939 Jack Kyker and Clarence Hicks, two cave guides who were exploring the cave on their own, found the remains of one of the cave's earliest visitors: a Pleistocene jaguar. Apparently, the jaguar entered the cave some twenty thousand years ago, lost his way in the darkness, and plunged to his death.

The owners of the cave at the time, Dr. W. J. Cameron and W. E. Michael of Sweetwater, submitted the bones of the jaguar and of another animal to the American Museum of Natural History in New York. The museum confirmed the bones had belonged to a large jaguar and an elk fawn. The following year George Gaylord Simpson, a vertebrate paleontologist from the museum, visited the site and recovered additional jaguar bones. He also made plaster casts of several jaguar footprints in the muddy floor of the cave and reported his findings, complete with photographs of the bones and footprints, in the August 1941 issue of the *American Museum Novitates.* Part of the collection of bones remains on display in the American Museum of Natural History in New York. The rest of the bones, along with plaster casts of the tracks, are now among the exhibits at the visitor center of the underground lake, known as the Lost Sea Adventure.

The cave's first visitors were not limited to jaguars and Cherokees, however. The first white settlers to arrive in the region around 1820 soon discovered that the cool, underground spaces provided a natural refrigeration system. With a constant temperature of fifty-eight degrees, Craighead Caverns were ideal for storing roots, potatoes, and other crops.

The cave also played a critical role during the Civil War as a source of saltpeter, a form of potassium nitrate used in the manufacture of gunpowder. Confederate soldiers mined the cave for the mineral around the clock to keep the Confederacy supplied with saltpeter for explosives. One diary of the era claims a Union spy attempted to blow up the entrance of the mining operation to prevent the saltpeter from making its way into the hands of Confederate forces. But the Confederate soldiers captured and shot the spy near a large gum tree at the cave entrance.

One soldier left behind a permanent mark in the cave, etching the date "1863" into one of the cave's walls with the carbon of his torch. The mark has been proven to be authentic through modern testing methods and is the earliest known date to exist in the caverns.

During the Prohibition years moonshiners discovered that the cave was a safe hiding place to set up their stills and make

Tennessee whiskey. Cockfighters joined in the fun as well, setting up cockpits for battling gamecocks. And in 1915 a developer saw the potential for profiting from public visitors. He purchased the caverns, installed a dance floor in one of the large rooms, and opened a tavern to attract guests who were fascinated by the idea of dining and dancing in a venue beneath the earth's surface.

In the 1920s the Tennessee Power Company from nearby Chattanooga worked with rural Sweetwater residents to cut poles from downed timber and provide the right-of-ways that would deliver electric service to the area. The company even installed a revolutionary lighting system in Craighead Caverns during the decade.

The moist, damp climate inside the depths of the earth also made the caverns the perfect place for growing mushrooms. A mushroom farm, located a few hundred feet from the entrance, operated in the cave from 1939 to 1940. Horses stabled at Fort Oglethorpe's Sixth Calvary, located in north Georgia, supplied manure for the underground farming operation.

A nightclub known as the Cavern Tavern operated in the cave during the late 1940s. With the cave's low altitude and high humidity, many partygoers did not realize the effects of liquor consumption in the depths of the cave until they staggered up to the entrance and reached the earth's surface. With the constant temperature of 58 degrees inside the cave, most people couldn't comprehend when they had had too much to drink until they reached sea level.

Today, tourists can enjoy the fascinating history of Craighead Caverns by taking the Lost Sea Adventure. Tour guides lead groups through the rooms where ancient jaguars roamed, moonshiners distilled whiskey, Confederates mined saltpeter, and Cherokees once gathered. Organized groups such as Scouts and schoolchildren can also take guided tours through undeveloped areas of the caverns by crawling through cracks and crevices. Since guests are certain to get muddy as they explore the off-the-beaten-track trails, they are advised to bring light jackets, long-sleeved shirts, old shoes, and an extra set of clean clothes for the trip home.

During the tours visitors can view stalactites, stalagmites, a waterfall, and rare, spiky crystalline formations called anthodites. These fragile clusters, commonly known as "cave flowers," are found in only a few of the world's caves. Craighead Caverns contains about half of the known formations in the world. These rare crystals, combined with the natural phenomenon of the underground lake, led the US Department of the Interior to declare the Lost Sea a registered National Natural Landmark in 1973, joining other distinct geological regions of the country to receive this designation, including Yosemite National Park in California and the Cape Hatteras National Seashore in North Carolina.

At the bottom of the cave is the Lost Sea. To reach the underground lake, visitors must walk down an incline about one-quarter mile in length. Glass-bottomed boats powered by electric motors are available for a seventy-five-minute tour of the lake, which is illuminated by underwater lights that line the perimeter. The lighting allows visitors to enjoy viewing some of the largest rainbow trout in North America. According to management, the trout were placed in the water as an experiment to see if the fish could find their way out of the lake. Apparently, the experiment failed, the trout reproduced, and the lake is now fully stocked with fish that have lost much of their color in their underground habitat. Fishing, however, is not permitted.

The visible portion of the Lost Sea covers four and one-half acres, measuring 800 feet long and 220 feet wide at normal "full" capacity. In times of extreme drought, the lake recedes significantly and visitors see a much larger cavern above the lake surface. During a severe drought in 2007 and 2008, for example, the water level in the lake dropped twenty-eight feet below its normal level, and the walkway and the boat dock were extended in order to continue to offer boat tours.

For many years the Lost Sea was considered the world's largest underground lake. With the discovery of Lake Vostok beneath the glaciers in Antarctica, measuring 160 miles long by 30 miles wide, the Lost Sea became recognized as the world's second-largest underground lake. It continues to hold the distinction of being listed in the *Guinness Book of World Records* as the largest underground lake in the United States.

The full extent of the Lost Sea is still not known, even though several teams of cave divers explored the underwater portion of the cave over a period of two years in the mid-1970s. Before making their first dives, the divers crawled around the dry portion of the caverns to see how the series of caves were laid out. Then they conducted the initial survey using one of the electric, glass-bottomed boats to cruise around the lake before plunging into the cool waters wearing full diving gear.

The divers carefully selected one of the many passages in the lake that had not yet been examined. To explore the depths of the lake, the cave divers knew they had to secure and tie off lines to guide them. Though they had no problems tying one end of a line to the underwater lights dangling about ten feet below the surface of the lake, finding a firm area to anchor the other end of the line was almost impossible. The fragile outcroppings of the walls and ceilings were far too delicate to hold the weight of the lines, and the floor of the lake consisted of fine silt made of red clay, often six feet thick, that wiggled as soon as they neared the bottom. At no point did they find a rocky floor to the lake.

They found the solution to their dilemma by driving six-foot stakes into the silt, working slowly and carefully so they would not stir up the red clay and diminish their visibility in the murky waters. Only twelve to eighteen inches of the stakes were visible after they worked them into the silt.

One weekend an employee of the US Geological Survey brought an underwater sonar unit to the site so the divers could measure the dimensions of the rooms in which they were swimming. With limited visibility and given the enormous size

COURTESY OF THE LOST SEA ADVENTURE, SWEETWATER, TENNESSEE

Visitors to the Lost Sea, America's largest underground lake, can take tours on glass-bottomed boats.

of the rooms, however, the sonar equipment failed to size up the area.

Though the divers were exploring an even larger series of rooms filled with water, they were unsuccessful in reaching the end of the cave. One limitation to their expedition was the massive amounts of silt clinging to the roof of the cave. Since they were exploring a passage that had never been touched by humans, clouds of silt rained down on them every time they exhaled. Occasionally, a few small rocks would also fall on them. At one point a boulder about the size of a small car fell from the ceiling, and the divers narrowly escaped being pinned.

After exploring more than thirteen acres of water, creating a map, and discovering significant changes in the water table, the divers ended their exploration of the measureless lake. Although no one knew where the lake ended, the divers had mapped out more than fifteen hundred feet of passage previously untouched by man. "We only explored one passage off of the lake," Jim Wyatt, one of the divers, later wrote. "It kept going and going, and we saw no need to look for other passages. My guess is that there are many more passages waiting to be explored."

More than fifty years passed between the time young Ben Sands stumbled onto the Lost Sea and the date that the underground lake in Craighead Caverns was rediscovered. When the Lost Sea opened for tours, Ben was honored as the first official visitor and was asked to choose the name for the site. Today, the Lost Sea and Craighead Caverns welcome thousands of tourists each year.

Undoubtedly, the remarkable Lost Sea and Craighead Caverns still hold secrets in their depths, secrets that are just waiting to be explored deep inside a mountain near the small town of Sweetwater in East Tennessee.

CHAPTER 3

The White Marble Mausoleum with Crimson Stains

C an a building mourn for its inhabitants? Is it possible for red streaks to appear in white marble, long after the stone slabs have been imported from Italy? Those are questions that continue to haunt the town of Cleveland, Tennessee, nearly a century after the tragic deaths of four members of one prominent family.

The Craigmiles family is at the very heart of the mystery that has long haunted the town of Cleveland, located in the southeast corner of Tennessee, a short distance north of Chattanooga.

The California gold rush of 1849 was in full swing when twenty-five-year-old John Henderson Craigmiles moved from Dalton, Georgia, to the town of Cleveland, Tennessee. Though John and his brother Pleasant M. Craigmiles were operating a profitable mercantile business in Cleveland during 1850, the promise of a rich future in the golden West was far too appealing for John to resist.

Unlike the majority of "forty-niners," however, prospecting for gold was not the focus of John's dreams. After arriving in California, the young man from Tennessee realized that prospectors in the booming western territory desperately needed supplies transported into the area from larger cities in the East. Convinced he could capitalize on fulfilling the needs of the constant stream of new arrivals in California, John purchased a fleet of six two-mast ships for shipping supplies between Panama and the West Coast. In addition to transporting cargo to California, he carried passengers from the eastern United States who had already booked passage to Central America and wanted to continue their journey to the golden West.

With his Midas touch, John struck gold with his shipping business, which prospered for several years until five of his ships were hijacked at sea. Mutinous crews made off with both the vessels and cargo, and claims from creditors wiped out John's fortune. Determined to rebuild his fortune with the one remaining ship from the fleet, John borrowed six hundred dollars from his brother Green Craigmiles. Within a short time he restored his wealth.

Once again a wealthy man, John returned to Cleveland, Tennessee, in 1857. He soon began courting Adelia Thompson, the daughter of local doctor Gideon Blackburn Thompson. Romance blossomed, and John and Adelia were married on December 18, 1860.

John's skills as a savvy businessman quickly became known throughout the South. As the winds of war swept through the country, the secretary of state for the Confederacy, Judah P. Benjamin, appointed John as the chief commissary agent for the South. Holding this position throughout the Civil War, John expanded his massive fortune by buying cattle, speculating in cotton, and selling goods to the Confederate Army at a large profit. He often bought meat at eight cents a pound and sold it for fourteen cents a pound as food for the Confederate troops. One source contends that he was drafted into the Confederate Army but used his wealth to his advantage by paying a substitute to serve in his place.

He was also wise enough to know that paper money was of little value and only traded in gold. After the defeat of the Confederacy, when the paper money printed in Richmond turned out to be worthless, John was in a much more financially stable condition than many other southern businessmen, who helplessly watched their fortunes vanish.

On August 4, 1864, Adelia gave birth to the couple's first child, Nina. The little girl became the center of the Craigsmiles' world. Protective of their daughter, John and Adelia hired tutors to teach Nina in the privacy of their home, even though the little girl had expressed a desire to attend school and enjoy the company of other children.

Dr. Thompson, Nina's maternal grandfather, often took his granddaughter on afternoon outings. On October 18, 1871, Dr. Thompson pulled his shiny black carriage in front of the Craigmiles' home for another outing with his precious Nina, who was now seven years old. Instead of the gentle mule that usually pulled the carriage, however, a black horse with a white blaze on its forehead stood in its place.

Was Adelia filled with a sense of foreboding when she realized that her father's customary mule had been replaced by a spirited horse? One version of the events of that fateful day contends that Adelia was reluctant to allow Nina to ride in the buggy pulled by the unfamiliar black horse, and conceded only when Dr. Thompson promised that he would not allow Nina to hold the reins.

As the buggy headed down the road and out of sight of the Craigmiles' home, no one would ever know the conversation that took place between the physician and his granddaughter. Did Nina plead with her grandfather to let her hold the reins? Was it impossible for the doting grandfather to deny the little girl's request? Or were they laughing so loudly as they approached the railroad crossing that they didn't hear the roar of a passing train?

At the last second Dr. Thompson pulled on the brake, but the terrified horse bolted toward the oncoming train. Dr. Thompson was thrown clear and survived the tragic accident, but Nina was hurled onto the tracks and instantly killed by the train.

John and Adelia were devastated by the loss. Two days later the town grieved with them during a memorial service at St. Alban's Episcopal Church. After the service Rev. George James wrote in St. Alban's historical register that the small town experienced a "thrill of horror" at the loss of the little girl.

The Craigmiles mausoleum sits behind Saint Luke's Episcopal Church in Cleveland, Tennessee.

Almost immediately John started making plans to build a church in memory of his daughter. On October 18, 1874, the third anniversary of Nina's death, Saint Luke's Episcopal Church opened to worshippers. The brick and stone structure was paid in full by the Craigmiles, who named the church in honor of the date of Nina's death and Saint Luke's Day, celebrated on October 18.

An alcove behind the pulpit, usually filled with floral arrangements, was originally designed to hold a bust of Nina. The Craigmiles family commissioned a sculptor to create the bust from white Italian marble, intending to place the work of art in "Nina's Niche." As the story goes, the sculpture never reached its destination in Cleveland, Tennessee, instead meeting its own tragic fate as part of the cargo aboard the HMS *Titanic*. Considering that the sinking of the *Titanic* occurred on April 15, 1912, more than forty years after little Nina's death, the story of the commissioned sculpture may be an exaggerated tale.

No sooner had the church been completed than the Craigmiles began planning the construction of another building on the lawn behind the church: a mausoleum for Nina's final resting place. Built with Carrara marble imported from Italy, the walls of the structure are four feet thick. A cross perches on a spire that rises more than thirty-seven feet high. Inside of the tomb Nina's remains rest in an ornate marble coffin designed by Italian sculptor Fabia Cotte.

Little Nina was not the sole occupant of the mausoleum for very long. Soon after Nina's body was interred in the mausoleum,

Adelia and John welcomed the birth of a son. Tragically, the infant lived only a few hours, and the Craigmiles placed the tiny body of the unnamed boy next to his sister in the mausoleum.

Not long after, children playing in the churchyard claimed they heard someone crying inside the marble structure. Then they noticed something equally strange and mysterious: Red streaks were forming on the white marble.

After losing both of their beloved children, John and Adelia must have thought that they had endured enough tragedies to last a lifetime. But tragic accidents claimed the lives of both husband and wife. On a cold January day in 1899, John Craigmiles slipped and fell on an icy street in Cleveland. He quickly developed an infection, followed by blood poisoning, and died a short time later. He was laid to rest in the mausoleum with his children. Years later, long after remarrying, Adelia was struck and killed by an automobile in September 1928 as she crossed Cleveland Street. She, too, joined her family in their final resting place inside the mausoleum.

According to the stories surrounding the mausoleum, the crimson streaks on the marble structure became more and more noticeable each time another member of Craigmiles family encountered a tragic death and was buried inside the building. Some local residents speculated that the marble itself was reacting to the tragedies, grieving for the family's losses and causing blood-red streaks around the door and mantel of the crypt.

Over the years, the crimson stains on the glistening marble have defied all explanations. Typically, a slab of imported Carrara marble does not have red streaks running through it. Moreover, neither natural elements nor chemicals have succeeded in washing away the red blotches marring the white stone.

Today, both Saint Luke's Episcopal Church and the Craigmiles' mausoleum are listed on the National Register of Historic Places. Visitors to the site can clearly see the blood-red marks on the white mausoleum behind the church.

CHAPTER 4

The Mystery of the Melungeons

Along the Virginia border in northeast Tennessee, settlers in Hancock and Hawkins Counties have been the subject of curiosity and mystery since the late 1700s. Even today, legends about the origin of this small group of people known as the Melungeons are under scrutiny by researchers and scientists who are determined to discover the true ancestry of this mysterious race.

Neither white nor black nor American Indian, Melungeons have never fit into any one category of race. Most Melungeons have dark-olive skin, high cheekbones, dark eyes, and thick, dark hair. Even the origin of name of *Melungeon* is controversial. Some say the word is a derivative of *mélange,* a French word meaning mixture, while others contend the name comes from the Grecian word *melas,* meaning "dark." *Melungo,* which means "sailor" in Afro-Portuguese, is another explanation for the name.

Since the pre–Revolutionary War era, the blending of Africans, American Indians, and Europeans has resulted in mixed ethnicities and races. Americans used terms such as "mulatto" to describe individuals with distinctive combinations of various racial characteristics. Before the Civil War the designation "mestee" was widely used in the United States for mixed-race individuals. Like the word *melungeon,* these terms share their roots in the Latin verb *miscere,* "to mix."

With physical characteristics resembling natives of Europe and the Mediterranean, many Melungeons believe they have roots in Portugal or Spain. One of the earliest legends contends that Melungeons are descendents of men who were members of Spanish exploration parties during the 1500s. The Spanish explorer Hernando de Soto, for example, ventured from Florida into parts of North Carolina and Tennessee in search of gold in 1540. According to this story, some of the men in de Soto's party became lost in the wilderness and were either captured or befriended by Cherokee Indians, intermarried with them, and left their descendents in Rhea, Hawkins, and Hancock Counties in Tennessee and neighboring counties in Virginia.

A second Spanish explorer, Juan Pardo, led several expeditions from present-day South Carolina into North Carolina and Tennessee during the 1560s. After establishing the first Spanish settlement in the interior of North Carolina, Pardo explored the Piedmont interior and Appalachian Mountains. Supposedly, hundreds of Spanish, Iberian, and Portuguese men disappeared from these expeditions, intermingled with Native American tribes, and became the source of the Western European, Turkish,

Moorish, and Portuguese characteristics so often seen in the physical features of their Melungeon descendents.

Ancestors of the Melungeons may also have been shipwrecked castaways. The legendary Sir Frances Drake planned to defeat his Spanish rivals in the New World with the help of more than five hundred captured Iberians, South American Indians, Berbers, Moors, Turks, and Muslims. But as he headed to the Caribbean with his shipload of captured warriors, a storm blew his ship off course and led him to the Roanoke colony. Documents report that more than four hundred of the captured soldiers disappeared. Did they flee inland, find a safe haven with native tribes, and take Native American women as wives to become the foundation of the mysterious Melungeon race? Perhaps they did. As early as 1673, English explorer James Needham reported that he had found Mediterranean-looking people living with Native American tribes in the wooded mountains of the New World and speaking broken sixteenth-century Elizabethan English.

More than one hundred years later, Revolutionary War veteran John Sevier, who would later become Tennessee's first governor, discovered that a "colony of dark-skinned, reddish-brown complexioned people" were living in the region that is now northeast Tennessee. They had European features, he reported, but were neither Native American nor Negro. And the colony had never taken part in Indian wars or beliefs, but cherished the cross, the symbol of Christianity.

The Melungeons also theorize that they are descendents of Portuguese sailors who arrived off the coast of North Carolina before the American Revolution and were attacked by hostile Native Americans. As the story goes, the sailors killed the Native American men, claimed the women as their own, and then proceeded to move westward through North Carolina.

Census, genealogical, and public records, including Revolutionary War land grants, during the last decade of the eighteenth century document that a substantial portion of residents living in the northeast corner of Tennessee and the surrounding region claimed to be of European descent. In the 1790 census, for instance, many people identified themselves as Portuguese, Portuguese-Indian, Black Dutch, French, and Spanish.

Other researchers theorize that the various Melungeon lines may have stemmed from the blending of black and white indentured servants living in Virginia in the mid-1600s, before slavery. As laws were established to condemn the mixing of races, these families could only intermarry with one another, and they migrated from Virginia through the Carolinas before settling in the mountains of East Tennessee.

The earliest documented reference to the term "Melungeon" was far from favorable, used in a derogatory manner in the September 26, 1813, minutes of Stoney Creek Baptist Church in Scott County, Virginia. During a church service Sister Susanna Kitchen complained against another church member "for saying she harbored them Melungins." The term appeared again

Howard Collins (1830–1906) and his daughter, Docia Collins, were members of a prominent Melungeon family in East Tennessee.

in October 1840 in Tennessee's *Jonesborough Whig,* where "an impudent Melungeon" from the nation's capital, then called Washington City, was identified as "a scoundrel who is half Negro and half Indian."

By all indications the word "Melungeon" became an offensive term, used by whites to belittle nonwhites with meager financial means and a low social status. In fact, most Melungeons resented the term and considered it to be an insult. Their true lineage, they insisted, was either Portuguese or Native American.

Throughout the nineteenth century the majority of Americans apparently assumed the dominant race in the mixed heritage of the Melungeons was black. This assumption even made its way into the laws of the land. In the Tennessee constitution of 1834, Melungeons were declared as "free men of color" and were denied the right to sue or testify. Unable to escape the chains of poverty and ostracized by whites, Melungeons took their case to the Tennessee Supreme Court before the Civil War. In the end the Supreme Court ruled in their favor, deciding Melungeons were not black and were entitled to send their children to school with white children.

Melungeons continued to learn that any connection with black ancestry prevented them from having the same privileges as whites, which may have been the reason they often claimed their ancestors were Portuguese. In 1874, for example, a court case in Tennessee challenged the inheritance of a Melungeon woman, Martha Simmerman. By law the woman would not be

MYTHS AND MYSTERIES OF TENNESSEE

entitled to the inheritance if she had an African heritage. Her attorney, Lewis Shepherd, argued successfully that Simmerman's family was descended from ancient Phoenicians who eventually migrated to Portugal and then to North America. Years later Shepherd wrote, "Our Southern high-bred people will never tolerate on equal terms any person who is even remotely tainted with negro blood, but they do not make the same objection to other brown or dark-skinned people, like the Spanish, the Cubans, the Italians, etc."

With the arrival of popular magazines in the 1890s, many fiction writers found a new audience for their tales of mountain life in the Appalachians and ignited a fascination with the mysterious race called the Melungeons. One Nashville writer in particular is credited with labeling the ancestry of the group as a "mystery," claiming they were a blend of African, white, and especially Native American and Portuguese ancestry. Even writers of nonfiction tried to trace the origins of the Melungeons, writing recollections of family history. And an 1894 government report from the US Department of the Interior called "Indians Taxed and Not Taxed" noted the Melungeons in Hawkins County "claim to be Cherokee of mixed blood."

By 1950 a scholarly dissertation on "Mixed-Blood Populations of the Eastern United States as to Origins, Localizations, and Persistence," by Edward Price, concluded that Melungeons had descended from free persons of color who moved into Hancock County in the late 1700s and early 1800s from the

Virginia–North Carolina Piedmont area. After thoroughly analyzing census and other archival records, Price determined that children of European and free black unions had intermarried with Native American descendents.

Nearly twenty years later another study by two cultural anthropologists, William S. Pollitzer and W. H. Brown, compared the physical characteristics and gene frequencies in six blood-group systems of 177 Melungeons in Tennessee and Virginia to various worldwide populations. Their conclusion was that the Melungeons most likely were derived from a predominately English background with some African-American and/or Cherokee roots, with a possible Portuguese component. The authors also concluded that the admixture from marriages with whites in recent generations was ending the ethnic distinctiveness of Melungeons. A review of this same study in 1990 argued that the Melungeons in the sample were a Caucasoid population from the Mediterranean, with some African ancestry.

Yet another study, composed in 1981 and based on extensive interviews in the region, concluded that the Melungeon identity as a distinctive mixed-race group had virtually disappeared. The author, anthropologist Anthony Cavender, stated that the term "Melungeon" now had two opposite meanings: a racial slur that still belittled people of low economic standing, and a term used by the local elites to identify themselves with an exotic, mysterious past.

The exotic, romantic association stemmed, in part, from tourism and promotion. Many Melungeons had become better educated over the years, increasing their economic status and earning a place in the middle and upper classes of society. With heightened media interest, local Melungeons seized the opportunity to promote their heritage and welcomed tourists to the community.

Law enforcement officers soon began wearing shoulder patches on their uniforms that declared Hancock County was the "Home of the Melungeons." An outdoor drama about Melungeons, "Walk towards the Sunset," drew scores of tourists to the area during the 1970s. Even local restaurants advertised "Melungeon cheeseburgers." In 2001 the Hancock County Chamber of Commerce website invited tourists to visit "Hancock County, Tennessee, home of the mysterious Melungeons." Plans called for the old county jail to be restored as a Melungeon history museum.

Still, others continued to debate the true ancestry of the Melungeons. By the end of the twentieth century, the publication of the book *The Melungeons: The Resurrection of a Proud People* renewed interest in the Portuguese lineage of the Melungeons. The author, Brent Kennedy, originally thought his ancestry was rooted in Ireland, Scotland, and Germany. But as he conducted genealogical research into his own family line, he was stunned to discover that his ancestors were Melungeons.

Kennedy theorized the Melungeons originated as Islamic Moors from Iberia, Turkey, and North Africa, refugees from

Spanish and English activities on the Atlantic coast in the 1500s. Masking themselves as Christian Portuguese to avoid possible ethnic cleansing, he asserted, the men made their way inland, intermarried to a limited degree with Native Americans, and created the people called Melungeons. Research into this theory is centered at the University of Virginia branch campus at Wise.

After publication of the book, Kennedy was diagnosed with a hereditary disease known as Familial Mediterranean fever, which is a common condition among Syrians and Turks. The experience convinced him that he must have Mediterranean roots. Why else would he have this genetic disorder?

A DNA study offered the best chance of finding an answer. Some Melungeons opposed it, more interested in leaving the past behind. Others hoped a study would prove that their roots were not tied to African ancestry. Still, Kennedy and other Melungeon leaders enlisted the help of Kevin Jones, a biologist at the University of Virginia's College at Wise, to conduct a DNA study.

With the help of a London geneticist, Jones looked at 120 DNA samples. He concluded that the roots of Melungeons are mostly Eurasian, spanning from Scandinavia to the Middle East. Some black and some Native American ancestry were also present in the samples.

The findings of another DNA study, released in 2012 in the *Journal of Genetic Genealogy,* concluded that Melungeons are the offspring of sub-Saharan African men and white women of northern or central European origins. Participants in the study were limited to sixty-nine male lines and eight female lines whose families were called Melungeon in the historical records of the 1880s and early 1900s in and around Tennessee's Hawkins and Hancock Counties. The study did not eliminate the possibilities of other racial mixing forming part of the Melungeon heritage.

Today, research continues on the factual origins of the Melungeons. With easy access to census records and other historical resources on the Internet, many individuals are researching their own family lines. For some, the Kennedy theory of Moorish ethnicity is accepted, while others believe their roots are a mixture of white, black, and Native American. One group of Melungeon descendants is actively seeking recognition as an Indian tribe from the state of Tennessee, continuing the claims of Cherokee and other Indian heritage.

In the end the history of the Melungeons may ultimately be the individual histories of many families, rather than of one people, according to one scholar. One researcher contends there is not a single racial or anthropological definition of *Melungeon* today. Some people simply identify themselves as such because of how they look or because they live in a former Melungeon community.

In 2001 the Hancock County Historical and Genealogical Society estimated that about five hundred Melungeon descendants still lived in northeast Tennessee and southwest Virginia. Another source contends that approximately forty communities similar to the Hancock County Melungeons live in the South. These communities are located in the Graysville area of Rhea and

Hamilton Counties and in Davidson and Wilson Counties in Tennessee, as well as in the states of Virginia, Kentucky, Florida, South Carolina, and Louisiana.

Who are the Melungeons? There may be as many as two hundred thousand descendents of the mysterious colony of olive-skinned people who lived for centuries in the foothills of the Appalachians. Moreover, each of their families may have different ethnic and racial identities, further complicating research and continuing to fuel the controversy over this mysterious group of people.

CHAPTER 5

The Legend of Davy Crockett

He was a simple man from Tennessee who became a legend in his own lifetime. And though his death occurred nearly two hundred years ago, Davy Crockett has become one of the most celebrated figures in American history, often rising to the status of a superhero of mythical proportion.

Who was Davy Crockett? According to some tall tales, he was the man who could wade the Mississippi, twist the tail off Halley's Comet, and slide down a thorny tree without a scratch. To baby boomers growing up during the 1950s, he came to life as actor Fess Parker in the television series and feature-length film *Davy Crockett: King of the Wild Frontier.*

The frontier lore swirling around the legendary hero Davy Crockett is actually based on the life of David Crockett, a frontiersman and congressman from Tennessee during the early 1800s. The real Crockett loved to spin his own tall tales and was prone to exaggerate his prowess as a hunter and an adventurer. His colorful personality attracted journalists like a magnet, and his life and stories became the inspiration for dozens of books, almanacs, songs, and films—most based on a mixture of fiction and fact.

A prime example of an exaggerated fact about Crockett starts with his birth. The first line of "The Ballad of Davy Crockett," popularized by the 1950s television series, claims he was "born on a mountaintop in Tennessee." In reality, David Stern Crockett was born in Greenville, Tennessee, on August 17, 1786. Current visitors to the Davy Crockett Birthplace State Historic Area in Greene County, Tennessee, are often disappointed to find that the closest mountaintop is about ten miles away from the site. And many people are even more surprised to discover that the real Crockett disliked being called Davy.

David's life of adventure began at an early age. In 1798 David's parents, John and Rebecca Crockett, opened a tavern on the road from Knoxville, Tennessee, to Abingdon, Virginia. Since money was always tight in the frontier household, John Crockett hired out his son to help drive a herd of cattle to Rockbridge County, Virginia. Twelve-year-old David dutifully fulfilled the contract, but the head of the cattle drive tried to detain him by force. The resourceful, rebellious young boy, however, escaped from the man's clutches and eventually returned home to Tennessee.

Once home, David attended school for a few months before discovering that playing hooky was much more fun than sitting in a schoolhouse. Knowing the elder Crockett would be furious at his son's rebellious ways, David ran away from home to escape his father's wrath. For the next two and a half years, he traveled from place to place, working at odd jobs.

By the time David returned home in 1802, he must have been ready to settle down. After finding work in the area, he began courting Margaret Elder, a young woman from nearby Dandridge, Tennessee. Though the couple took out a license to marry on October 21, 1805, Margaret jilted her fiancé to marry another man. David later said he was heartbroken over the loss.

Less than one year later, David married Mary "Polly" Finley in Jefferson County, Tennessee, and the couple began their life together in East Tennessee. Their first son, John Wesley, was born in 1807, followed by William in 1809. Two years later, David's restless spirit and desire to find richer land for farming led the family to pack up their worldly goods and move west about 150 miles to Lincoln County, Tennessee.

Though the Lincoln County farmland was not as rich as David had hoped, the abundance of game in the region was beyond his expectations. During this time of his life, David earned his reputation as a skilled marksman and hunter. Hunting and killing bear was his primary claim to fame. "The Ballad of Davy Crockett" claims Davy "killed him a b'ar when he was only three. . . ." Obviously, David was a skilled bear hunter at an early age, but becoming a marksman at the tender age of three was part of his mythical legend.

David and Polly soon moved again, this time to Franklin County, Tennessee. Between 1813 and 1815 David volunteered for service against the Creek Indians, serving as a scout and searching for Indians in Alabama and Florida for several months at a time. When he returned home in 1815, he was delighted that a new addition to the family, Margaret, had arrived during his absence. Sadly, his wife Polly died the summer after Margaret's birth. No records have been found to indicate the cause or exact date of her death.

He quickly found a new wife, Elizabeth Patton, to help him raise his children and was elected to serve as a lieutenant in the thirty-second militia regiment of Franklin County. Always restless, David explored Alabama with an eye toward settlement. But during his exploration, the frontiersman caught malaria, most likely contracted during his search for Creek Indians in the swampy waters of Florida. Back home in Tennessee, his family was told he'd died from the disease. But to their astonishment, David recovered and returned home to his family. Surviving malaria only enhanced his legendary status in later years.

In September 1817 the Crocketts settled in the territory soon to become Lawrence County, Tennessee, at the head of Shoal Creek. David quickly took an active role in the frontier town, assuming the position of Justice of the Peace and Commissioner of Lawrenceburg. He was also named colonel of the Thirty-seventh Militia Regiment and proudly retained the title of "Colonel Crockett" for the rest of his life.

Impressed by David's likeable nature, natural good humor, and involvement in local affairs, friends and neighbors urged him to

Portrait of David Crockett by S.S. Osgood, circa 1830s.

PHOTO COURTESY OF TENNESSEE STATE LIBRARY AND ARCHIVES

run for higher office on the state level. On January 1, 1821, David resigned as commissioner to run for a seat in the Tennessee state legislature as the representative for Lawrence and Hickman Counties.

With no formal education, David Crockett had never run a political campaign. By his own admission, he knew little about politics or governmental affairs. The mere thought of speaking in front of large crowds made him nervous. Still, the idea of running for office appealed to him, and he threw his hat into the ring for the state legislature.

During the summer of 1821, David participated in speaking engagements throughout the two counties he hoped to represent. At political rallies he keenly observed that the crowds grew weary of his long-winded opponents who would speak for hours on end. Patiently waiting until all of his rivals had addressed the crowds, David would step up, tell a funny story or a single joke, and offer to treat the crowd to a round of drinks at the bar. This sly political tactic stole the hearts of the voters, who could identify with him. After all, he was one of their own—an uneducated, hardworking family man.

He also played up his reputation as a bear hunter, which gave him an aura of fearlessness and independence, during his campaigns. Over time, legends about Davy Crockett claimed he could stare a bear into submission and that his grin could stun raccoons and knock the bark off trees.

In August 1821 David won the election by more than a two-to-one vote. His career as a legislator began the next month in the Fourth Tennessee General Assembly. He absorbed as much as he could of political issues of the day and advocated for landholders and squatters in West Tennessee. He was reelected to the seat in 1823.

Though David's first bid for a congressional seat in 1825 ended in defeat, he successfully defeated two opponents and was elected to the US House of Representatives in 1827. He was reelected for a second term in 1829, but hopes for a third term were dashed when he opposed many of President Andrew Jackson's policies, particularly the Indian Removal bill that would relocate Native Americans from their homeland in Tennessee to new lands in the West.

After narrowly losing his bid for reelection in 1831, David returned home to Tennessee as an unemployed congressman. During this time he began to dispense his no-nonsense, practical advice with the expression, "Be sure you're right. Then go ahead." The saying eventually became known as the motto of David Crockett of Tennessee.

But as David farmed, hunted, and borrowed money to build up a war chest for his next political campaign, the American public and press had not forgotten him. In spite of his political defeat, David Crockett and his image continued to fascinate Americans. And between 1831 and 1833, a New York play and a book based on the life of David Crockett catapulted him into a national personality.

First, the play, *The Lion of the West,* opened in New York City. Produced by James Kire Paulding, the theatrical show featured the antics of an uneducated frontier colonel, Nimrod Wildfire. Newspapers were quick to report that Crockett had inspired the play, and theatergoers found enough similarities between David and Nimrod to make the connection. The highly exaggerated account of David's life helped to cement his legendary life in the public's imagination.

Moreover, any distinction between fact and fiction was banished on the evening when David Crockett attended a benefit performance in Washington, D.C., that highlighted some scenes from *The Lion of the West.* A hush fell over the audience as Nimrod Wildfire stepped up to the footlights and bowed to David Crockett, who was seated in a special theater box near the stage. David, in turn, rose and bowed to the actor. The crowd went wild, clapping and cheering for both the fictitious and real versions of David Crockett.

Then, in January 1833, a book, *Life and Adventures of Colonel David Crockett of West Tennessee,* was published. Though the book included true episodes from David's life, it also contained some tall tales that portrayed him as a crude, uneducated backwoodsman.

David was far from pleased with the unauthorized biography. During his political career, he had tried to detach himself from the stereotypical image of an ignorant backwoodsman who possessed few, if any, social graces. For the most part, he had succeeded. In newspapers and magazines of the 1830s, he was known as Colonel Crockett, a distinction that David proudly accepted. The New York *Sun* described him as "a gentleman, his speech flashing with wit, but never vulgar or buffoonish." And one man remembered David as "a pleasant, courteous, and interesting man, who though uneducated in books, was a man of fine instincts and intellect."

Even his manner of dress was part legend, part truth. David wore a buckskin shirt only to reinforce his image on the campaign trail, and he may never even have owned a coonskin hat. Away from Tennessee and his familiar hunting grounds, David did not dress as a backwoodsman. As a congressman, he was "never attired in a garb that could be regarded as differing from that worn by gentlemen of his day—never in coonskin cap or hunting shirt," recalled William L. Foster, the son of Senator Ephraim Foster.

Still, the massive publicity surrounding David Crockett may have helped him win reelection to Congress in 1833. And the publication of his authorized autobiography in 1834 continued to capture the public's imagination. In fact, numerous books and almanacs about Davy Crockett were published over the next two decades. Though they claimed to contain true stories about David Crockett, frontiersman and politician, most of the stories were actually the fictional adventures of a larger-than-life frontier superman, a legend who could whip his weight in wildcats.

With Crockett's status as a living folk hero, the image of his physical appearance loomed larger than life. Most historians believe that David had brown hair, blue eyes, rosy cheeks, and stood about five feet, eight inches tall, which was tall for the period. But in the public's eyes, he stood as tall as a mythical giant who could perform supernatural feats. In several historical accounts witnesses described him as "tall in stature," "about six feet high," and weighing about two hundred pounds. "His hair was long, dark, and curly looking, rather uncombed than carefully attended to," one newspaper reported.

To most historians, David Crockett was a popular yet ineffective politician during the early 1800s. His record in Congress was less than stellar, considering that most of the legislation he favored failed to pass. After losing his congressional seat once again in the 1835 election, David knew that his political days were numbered, and he bluntly told his Tennessee neighbors that he was finished with politics. "I concluded my speech by telling them that I was done with politics for the present, and that they might all go to hell, and I would go to Texas," he reportedly said.

True to his word, David left Tennessee in November 1835 for East Texas. Though controversy swirled around the reason for his departure from his beloved Tennessee, his restless nature may have prompted him to explore the uncharted region for a new place to settle.

Whatever the reason for going to Texas, David Crockett knew that war with Mexico was inevitable, and he deliberately chose to arrive at San Antonio in time for Mexico's General Santa Anna to launch an attack on the Alamo Mission. David Crockett reportedly died on March 6, 1836, fighting at the Alamo during the Texas war for independence.

But the death of David Crockett, just as his birth and life, remained controversial. Initial reports claimed that David and a few others survived the siege on the Alamo but were later executed on the orders of General Santa Anna. A Mexican soldier's diary, translated and published in 1975, confirmed this version of David's death.

Still, the true account of David's last moments at the Alamo vanished with rumors and speculation in the decades after his death. One report claimed that David had been captured and was sentenced to forced labor in a Mexican mine. For years following the battle, newspapers reported numerous sightings of him in Mexico.

After David's passing, the legends became more absurd, mixing tall tales and half-truths about his life and death. Books, plays, and even musical scores such as "Colonel Crockett's March" became more popular than ever before.

Renewed interest in the legend of Davy Crockett exploded in the 1950s owing to the creativity of Walt Disney and the arrival of the new medium of television in the homes of the baby-boomer generation. *Disneyland,* a weekly hour-long show that aired on Wednesday evenings on ABC, launched a series about American folk heroes in late 1954. The first installment featured a three-part series focused on David Crockett.

Davy Crockett: Indian Fighter, was beamed over the airwaves on December 15, 1954; *Davy Crockett Goes to Congress* was broadcast on January 26, 1955; and *Davy Crockett at the Alamo* appeared on February 23, 1955. Later in 1955 the three hours of the miniseries were reworked for release in movie theaters as a feature-length film called *Davy Crockett: King of the Wild Frontier.*

The "Crockett craze" was one of the biggest events of the decade. Across America a previously unknown actor named Fess Parker came to life as Davy Crockett on television and the big screen. Walt Disney, who had spotted Fess in a small science-fiction thriller, thought he would be perfect for the part of Crockett. Audiences agreed.

Two more television shows, *Davy Crockett's Keelboat Race* and *Davy Crockett and the River Pirates,* were broadcast on ABC in November and December 1955. The following year the two television shows were combined and released to theaters as *Davy Crockett and the River Pirates.*

The background score to the television series and feature-length movies, "The Ballad of Davy Crockett," fueled the Crockett craze. The simple tune eventually was recorded in sixteen versions by various vocalists, with sales reaching four million copies. Ironically, the ballad was composed as an afterthought, inserted into the television series to help fill the sixty-minute slots of each episode.

Soon department stores were stocking three thousand items in special Crockett sections, selling everything from frontier apparel to ladies' panties. But the coonskin cap was the most popular item, helping to fulfill countless American children's desires to become part of the Davy Crockett legend.

To the American public, Davy Crockett was an admirable, real-life hero and a powerful role model for children of the 1950s. On the big screen he always lived up to his motto of doing what's right—even though Hollywood often stretched the truth to emphasize his character's high standards. In one scene Davy stood up in Congress to defend the human rights of Indians, and his fierce opposition to Jackson's Indian Removal bill cost him his congressional career. In reality, Congressman Crockett tried to remain quiet on his opposition to the Indian Removal bill, knowing his constituents in Tennessee favored removal. Word spread of his opposition, however, and he lost the election.

Historians contend that John Wayne's portrayal of Davy Crockett in *The Alamo,* the 1960 film from United Artists, was a good representation of the real David Crockett—a straight shooter and a man of his word who was always quick to act on his promises (or threats). John Wayne, a big man, standing more than six feet tall, may have towered over the real David Crockett in height. But Davy Crockett's powerful legacy left no doubt with his adoring public that he was a man tall in both stature and character.

Famed as a frontiersman, folk hero, congressman, and Alamo defender, Davy Crockett was one of the most celebrated and mythologized figures in American history. Crockett's biographers often say there were actually two Crocketts: David, the frontiersman and congressman martyred at the Alamo, and Davy, the larger-than-life folk hero whose exploits were glorified in several books and a series of almanacs.

Clearly, David Crockett was an outstanding frontiersman, a colorful congressman, and a true American hero who died in the act of defending his country at the Alamo. But it is the *legend* of the invincible Davy Crockett—an intriguing mixture of tall tale and half-truth sprinkled with occasional facts—that will continue to endure for generations.

CHAPTER 6

The Ghost of Brinkley Female College

At age thirteen Clara Robertson was considered an ideal student at Memphis's Brinkley Female College. The daughter of a local attorney, young Clara attended church regularly with her family, took her studies seriously, and practiced her piano religiously. But on Tuesday, February 21, 1871, Clara encountered a sight that would forever change her life.

As Clara practiced her music lessons in one of the upper rooms of the two-story building known as Brinkley Female College, a ghost suddenly appeared before her. Through Clara's eyes, it seemed as though she were gazing upon the apparition of a young girl, about the age of eight, with hollow, dull eyes and a mournful expression on her gaunt face. The young girl was wearing a threadbare, dirty dress of faded pink covered with splotches of green, slimy mold.

Horrified by the sight, Clara leaped up, darted into another room, and jumped into bed. The ghostly form followed close behind, silently crept up to the bedside and laid a bony hand on the pillow. Clara, who must have been too frightened to speak, motioned for the object to go away. The ghost finally disappeared through the door.

Clara immediately relayed the story to her classmates and teachers. Most of the students—between forty and fifty young ladies—were terrified by the tale. But a minority of girls reacted with skepticism, mocking Clara with such cruelty that the young victim broke down in tears. The teachers at the school doubted the story as well.

At home that evening Clara's father insisted the incident must have been the work of a few classmates who were playing a cruel joke on her. He also maintained that she could not stay home from school and miss her studies the next day.

Wednesday passed uneventfully at school, and Clara resumed her studies. On the following day, however, another frightful event occurred as Clara practiced her piano lessons in the company of two other students in the music room on the upper floor of the building. All of the girls were startled by a splashing sound similar to water spilling onto the floor. As they looked in the direction of the sound, the strange visitor appeared once again. Clara distinctly saw the ghostly apparition, though the other two girls later said they saw something more like a shadowy figure. Once again, Clara told the story to her classmates, teachers, and family. And once again, most were skeptical of the incident.

The following week the ghost appeared in the music room for a third time. Determined to find a credible witness to the sight, Clara ran down the steps and asked Miss Jackie Boone, one of the teachers, to return to the music room with her. When they stepped into the room, Clara could see the figure in detail. Miss Boone, however, saw the figure "imperfectly," according to one account. When the teacher encouraged Clara to address her strange visitor, the young girl asked, "Why are you here? And what do you want?"

The ghost gestured toward the window and explained that some valuables were located beneath a stump about fifty yards from the house, and she wanted Clara to have them. After the object finished speaking, she suddenly vanished. Though Clara and another student clearly heard the ghost's words, Miss Boone later claimed that she only heard gruff noises.

That evening Clara told her father, attorney J. R. Robertson, about the day's events. The following day, Mr. Robertson visited the director of the institution, Mr. Meredith, and his wife, to discuss the issue. Though the Merediths believed a practical joker was responsible for the strange occurrences, they agreed to conduct an investigation of the matter.

While the director and his wife assembled the students in a hallway to question them about the incidents, they instructed Clara to wait outside the house. But as soon as Clara stepped into the yard, the apparition appeared a few feet in front of her. Although Clara started to scream, the ghost told her not to be frightened. "My name is Lizzie," the vision said gently. "I will not hurt you."

Terrorized, Clara stood motionless as the ghost explained what she wanted. The Brinkley college property was rightfully hers, the visitor insisted. She had been the last member of the family to pass away, so no one else could claim it. The current owners did not have legal title to the property—and she wanted Clara to claim the property in her own name by retrieving the documents buried in the yard.

Puzzled by the unexplainable turn of events, Mr. Robertson discussed the situation with a legal client at his office. The client, a spiritual medium by the name of Mrs. Nourse, offered to visit Clara and see if she could comprehend the situation.

Later that evening at the Robertsons' home, several neighbors gathered around a table with Clara and her father as Mrs. Nourse prepared to conduct a séance. Though Mr. Robertson and most of his neighbors had never believed in ghosts or spirits, they were astonished by the events that unfolded before them.

Clara swooned and fell back into her chair. Her eyes remained open in a vacant stare as she hurled her hands back and forth in a violent manner. Mr. Robertson grasped his daughter's hands so she would not harm herself, and Clara became much calmer.

She remained silent as the medium placed a pencil in her hand and a piece of paper on the table. Wordlessly, she began to write down answers to the group's questions. Under what stump were the valuables buried? Clara instantly wrote the reply: Under the stump where the ghost had stood in the schoolyard, five feet under the ground. Why did the vision choose Clara to possess the property? The answer: The problem had long burdened the ghost, and by revealing the solution to Clara, her spirit was now free. The ghost also warned that the papers must be recovered immediately or someone else would take possession of them.

Further details of the hidden valuables were also revealed that evening. The spirit informed the group that the buried treasure consisted of several thousand dollars, jewelry that included valuable diamonds, and the title papers of the estate. Moreover, the ghost revealed her name was Lizzie Davidson. In closing she wrote, "Good night. Kiss Clara, for I love her."

As soon as Mrs. Nourse kissed Clara on the cheek, the young girl sat up and rubbed her eyes. Totally unaware of the strange events that had just transpired, she informed the group that she had been sleeping. Several of the gentlemen immediately left the house and headed to the college, determined to excavate the stump and find the buried treasure.

Word of Clara's ghostly sightings spread rapidly throughout Memphis. Within days, the headlines of the *Memphis Avalanche* newspaper proclaimed, "Brinkley Female College Haunted in an Uproar of Terror and Confusion."

Several stories about the ghost ran in the *Memphis Avalanche,* fueling the imagination of Memphis residents. During an interview with a *Memphis Avalanche* reporter, Mr. Meredith suggested that Clara had been hallucinating. Though he praised Clara's character, behavior, and trustworthiness, he expressed concern over the consequences to the school from the negative publicity. He even speculated that the ghost story was a hoax concocted by the headmasters of competing schools to drive Brinkley Female College out of business. Moreover, he insisted, the two girls with Clara were no longer certain that they had seen the vision. Now they were questioning their memories of the mysterious appearance of the ghost, wondering if the ghostly figure had only been a figment of their imaginations.

Mr. Meredith also revealed that several people had warned him that the old Brinkley mansion was haunted before he had moved into the building. During the first few months of his residency, he heard strange noises at night. But he later discovered the source of the racket had been nothing more than a raccoon roaming through the building.

The same *Avalanche* reporter also interviewed Mr. Robertson, who admitted Clara's story was hard to believe in the beginning. But Clara was a healthy, intelligent girl who had recently joined the church, and he felt obligated to find out more about the mysterious series of events surrounding his daughter.

As news swept through the city that diggers were excavating the yard of Brinkley Female College in search of buried treasure, hundreds of people flocked to the grounds to witness the sight. Under the pale ghostly light of the moon, the crowds watched the men dig into the ground with shovels, picks, and spades. The darkness gave way to dawn, and still the digging continued. Once the stump was removed, the diggers found some mortared bricks in the shape of an arch, but the buried treasure remained hidden from view.

On Sunday Clara dutifully attended church. Monday passed uneventfully until the evening hours. In the backyard of her home with a young friend around nine o'clock, Clara was startled by the sudden appearance of the ghost of Brinkley College. Her companion, frightened by Clara's screams, darted away before she could catch a glimpse of the uninvited guest. The ghost reprimanded Clara for not finding the treasure and urged her to find it. If she didn't hurry, the ghost insisted, others would be the first to discover the secret.

Though it was late in the evening, Clara knew that the excavation of the school grounds was still under way. She quickly headed to Brinkley Female College, accompanied by a neighbor, Miss Franklin.

At the school the spirit appeared to Clara again. She pointed toward a specific area of the excavation and insisted Clara alone must dig for the treasure. Clara carefully stepped into the hole, turned over one spade of dirt, leaned forward as if to pick something up, and fainted.

After being carried into the house, Clara quickly came to her senses and stated that she was just about to pick up the jar when she fell into a stupor. Seeing Clara's dismay, Mrs. Nourse, the medium, offered to conduct another séance.

The spirit of Lizzie soon appeared. This time, she identified herself as the spirit of Lizzie Davie, rather than Davidson.

The medium informed Lizzie that Clara was too nervous to dig for the treasure and asked if her father could retrieve the treasure in Clara's place. Lizzie agreed but with one stipulation: The jar should not be opened for sixty days. She also said the jar would be found under the brick arch.

Mr. Robertson, accompanied by the medium and two diggers, followed the direction of the spirit. After digging an hour around the brickwork, he found a glass jar, which he quietly passed to the medium. Though the unopened jar was covered with mold, several bags and packages and a yellowed envelope could be seen through the glass.

A jubilant crowd followed Mr. Robertson to his residence, anxious to see if he would open the jar. Mr. Robertson, however, vowed to wait sixty days before unveiling the jar's contents, as the spirit had instructed. Young Clara was simply grateful her father had finally unearthed the treasure, hoping the visits from ghostly Lizzie would come to an end.

But the frenzy over the ghostly tale was far from finished in Memphis. As the city impatiently waited for the sixty days to end, Memphians held séances of their own and indulged in spirits of a different kind, drinking "ghost cocktails" at every social opportunity. Mr. Robertson generously offered to open the "Brinkley College Ghost Jar" in public at the Greenlaw Opera House and devote the proceeds of admission to the church orphanage.

During the two-month waiting period, older residents of the city also had the chance to recall the family named Davie who had lived in the mansion that eventually became known as Brinkley Female College. Colonel Davie had built the mansion as a residence for his family in 1855. One of the daughters, Lizzie, died at home in 1860. Remembered as a beautiful child with long, dark hair and dark eyes, Lizzie was described as an intelligent, sweet girl who passed away around the age of seven or eight.

The older citizens of Memphis also recalled one unusual fact about the child's funeral. Instead of being buried in a traditional white shroud, Lizzie had been buried in a pink dress with white trim and pink slippers. Moreover, a scandalous lawsuit over the land on which the mansion had been built occurred about the same time.

The revelations about the first owners of the Brinkley building, the chancery lawsuit over the land, and the young girl who had died in the mansion only fueled the firestorm of speculation about the "Brinkley ghost" to new heights. Memphis citizens were soon referring to the ghost as "Pink Lizzie" and debating the possibilities of a supernatural spirit revealing long-forgotten secrets to a young girl. How could Clara have known Lizzie's name? Did Clara realize Lizzie was buried in a pink dress instead of a white shroud? Did someone tell Clara about a property dispute that ended up as a scandalous lawsuit? Was all of it mere coincidence? Or had Pink Lizzie's spirit revealed herself to Clara to find some peace with the past?

As the community debated the issues, Mr. Robertson was still planning to open the mysterious jar in public at the

Greenlaw Opera House. But one evening, several days before the scheduled event, he heard some noises and conversation in the backyard of his residence. Politely excusing himself from the company of guests sitting in the parlor, he went outside to investigate the sounds. Seeing nothing out of the ordinary, Mr. Robertson headed toward an outhouse on the grounds. But just as he stepped up to the door, two men rushed up to him. One of the men pointed a pistol in his face and warned him that they would kill him if he uttered a sound.

The two men marched Mr. Robertson to a small stable in the rear of the property, where another pair of men waited for them. "We have come after that jar," one man said, "and you have got to tell us where it is or we'll kill you."

Fearing for his life, Mr. Robertson instructed them to look under the seat in the outhouse. As two of the men retreated to the outhouse, the remaining pair of thugs pointed pistols at Mr. Robertson's head and threatened to kill him if he made a sound.

Within a few minutes the men returned with the jar in hand. One man grasped Mr. Robertson's throat, choking him, while another man struck him in the head with his pistol.

A house servant, concerned about Mr. Robertson's absence, left the house to look for the attorney and soon found him lying in a pool of blood near the stable. Several of the houseguests helped the servant carry Mr. Robertson into the house and called for a physician to examine his head wounds.

When Mr. Robertson gained consciousness, he recalled the incident with vivid detail, even remembering that one man with light hair and a pale complexion had been wearing dark clothes.

In spite of the victim's detailed descriptions of his assailants, the culprits were never found, and the jar and its contents were never recovered. Still, the story of the Brinkley ghost became a local legend, and Mr. Robertson wrote a book, *The Brinkley Female College Ghost Story,* that recounted the tale.

As Mr. Meredith predicted, enrollment plummeted at the Brinkley Female College as a result of all the media attention on the school, and the institution soon closed. Clara eventually married a spiritualist and was known for conducting séances in her later years.

The building that once housed the Brinkley Female College was divided into apartments and used as rental property until it was demolished in 1972. And though Clara and the school building no longer exist, the legend of the ghost of the Brinkley Female College continues to live in the true spirit of local lore.

CHAPTER 7

The Haunted Hales Bar Dam

T hirty miles west of Chattanooga, Tennessee, the partial remains of an abandoned dam on the Tennessee River occupy an area that was once Cherokee Indian territory. Some believe the spirits of the Indians who once lived there may still linger today in the waters of the mighty Tennessee, haunting the ghostly ruins of Hales Bar Dam in Marion County, Tennessee.

In 1775 three Cherokee chiefs agreed to sell more than twenty million acres of land in present-day Kentucky and Tennessee to white settlers. Part of this land included a turbulent thirty-mile stretch of the Tennessee River, running from Chattanooga in Hamilton County to neighboring Marion County. Well known for the perilous whirlpool in a mountainous gorge known as the "Suck," this stretch of river was considered the most dangerous part of the entire 652 miles of the Tennessee River. Suck Creek, an untamed mountain stream, often added to the force of the whirlpool by discharging vast quantities of rock, logs, and debris into the river.

Cherokee warrior Chief Dragging Canoe fought against surrendering more land to the white man and proclaimed that the area would become "a dark and bloody ground." Determined to drive the settlers from Cherokee lands, Dragging Canoe and several young Creek and Cherokee warriors formed the Chickamauga confederation. Calling themselves the Chickamauga Cherokees, they proceeded to lead violent attacks on white settlements in the region.

Dragging Canoe and his people were well aware of the dangers of the turbulent Suck. One of their legends gives vivid descriptions of the haunted whirlpool, including the consequences of venturing too close to the dangerous waters. According to the legend, two Cherokee braves in a canoe on the Tennessee River spotted circles of swift-moving waters ahead of them. Intending to wait for the currents to subside, they paddled their canoe to the banks of the river. But the whirlpool expanded and intensified, sucking them into the circling waters.

The force of the water tossed the men out of the canoe and carried them into the depths of the river. A huge fish seized one of the men, who disappeared from sight and was never seen again. The whirling waters tossed the second man in circles, spinning him into the depths of the currents until he was caught by another current that pitched him into shallow water. The man struggled ashore and survived the ordeal.

Afterward the man recalled the horrors of the experience. When he reached the inner depths of the whirlpool, he could

Local legends claim that ghostly spirits haunt the abandoned Hales Bar Dam in Marion County, Tennessee.

PHOTO COURTESY OF THE AUTHOR

look down as though he were looking through the roof of a house. There, on the bottom of the river, he saw a crowd of people with outstretched arms, beckoning him to join them. But just as their hands reached out to grasp him, a strong current tugged him away and pulled him back from their grasp.

Soon, boatmen along the Tennessee River became vividly aware of the dangerous eight-mile stretch known as the Suck. Like the Cherokees in the legend, the men who piloted vessels through the area kept a close eye on the water and heeded the warnings of the Indian tale. If they noticed sudden eruptions in the currents, they tied up their vessels along the riverbanks to wait for quieter waters.

News about the perils of the Suck spread far beyond the region. Although Thomas Jefferson never saw the Suck, he mentioned the dangerous waters in his book *Notes on the State of Virginia.* The Virginia statesman noted that it "takes in trunks of trees or boats, and throws them out again half a mile below."

Despite the increasing knowledge of the river's dangers among white settlers, some travelers were not quite as fortunate as the brave who survived the clutches of the Suck. Moreover, Dragging Canoe's braves staked out the area in hopes of seizing every opportunity for revenge against the white people who kept encroaching upon their land.

One of the most unfortunate sagas in Tennessee's history occurred during a river trip through the area in 1780. Colonel John Donelson led a flotilla of thirty to forty boats filled with about three hundred people over the Tennessee River, headed for the new settlement of Nashborough. Among the travelers was Donelson's young daughter, Rachel, who later married Andrew Jackson.

One March evening the group made an early camp along the river in present-day Hamilton County, where one of the women gave birth to the first white baby on record in the county's historical accounts. The following day the flotilla resumed the trip, winding their way through Chattanooga and into the mountain gorge. Though they thought the Indians trailing behind in their canoes were making friendly gestures, they soon discovered they were being ambushed. The Indians seized the last boat, sailing at the rear of the fleet due to an outbreak of smallpox among the passengers, and killed or captured all of the twenty-eight people onboard.

As the fleet pushed forward into the Suck, Dragging Canoe's men relentlessly followed the boats. A vessel carrying personal possessions overturned in the rough waters. As Donelson's party stopped at the riverbanks to recover some of the cargo, Indians perched on the cliffs above them opened fire and wounded several passengers.

Another boat ran into rocks at the Suck and became stuck. Though the Indians shot several people and captured two of the passengers, the woman who had given birth the previous day jumped into the water and pushed the boat away from the boulders. Her baby, however, did not survive the ordeal.

Though Donelson's flotilla resumed their journey and successfully reached their destination in Middle Tennessee, Dragging Canoe remained the ruler of the Tennessee River, ambushing settlers and making river travel dangerous. And long after Dragging Canoe's death in 1792, the Suck continued to torment travelers. Several craft disappeared in the clutches of the spiraling whirlpool, as did people and livestock.

By 1830 the US government was advised to improve the section of river. But it wasn't until 1900 that the idea of building a dam came to light. Josepheus Conn Guild, a young Tennessee engineer, worked with the US Army Corps of Engineers to develop a plan that would not only tame the river but harness the waters to provide energy to Tennessee.

In 1904 an Act of Congress granted permission for the construction of the first multipurpose lock-and-dam system along the Tennessee River at an estimated cost of three million dollars. Moreover, the Chattanooga and Tennessee River Power Company became the first private company to be permitted to construct a dam over a large, navigable river. Although several dams were erected in Tennessee during the first decades of the twentieth century, they were built on smaller rivers and did not include facilities to aid in navigation.

Work began in October 1905 on property belonging to George Hale, and the facility under construction was named in honor of the Hale family. A workforce of about five hundred men labored night and day, six days a week, with large steam shovels, masonry machinery, and concrete mixers to build the project.

To accommodate the large workforce, a village literally grew overnight on both sides of the river. Cottages, a hotel, and even a baseball park cropped up on the hillsides overlooking the river, and the little town was named Guild in honor of the engineer who launched the project. At the peak of construction, some fourteen hundred employees worked on the dam.

But construction of the lock and dam proved to be much more difficult than anyone had anticipated. The foundation of the dam rested on limestone, which eroded quickly with the constant flow of water. With cost overruns rapidly mounting, the original contractor abandoned the project in 1907. Other contractors under consideration refused to finish the job.

Was Dragging Canoe's curse at work? Some speculated that the white man's attempt to control the river and land that once belonged to the Cherokee was doomed from the start.

It took several more firms to finish the project, but Hales Bar Lock and Dam was finally completed in 1913 after eight years of construction. At that time it was one of the largest hydroelectric projects in the United States and had the highest locks in the world, with a capability of lifting boats to a height of forty-one feet. The final cost of approximately ten million dollars far exceeded the original estimate of three million.

But the dam continued to leak relentlessly. In an ongoing attempt to prevent leaks, workers known as the "Rag Gang" stuffed heavy rags, old carpets, and strips of mesh into the gaping crevices.

To accommodate the growing population of workers and their families, the Hales Bar School was built in 1922. Children who lived on the west bank of the river had to travel across the river in a dimly lit, damp tunnel that ran underneath the dam. Once they arrived on the east side of the river, the children made their way up spiral steps and walked through the powerhouse and on to the school house. The narrow tunnel served as common passage for the workers and children on a daily basis.

The Tennessee Valley Authority took over operations of the dam in 1939 and spent millions of man hours and dollars in efforts to control the leakage through the porous limestone and portions of the concrete dam. After nearly three decades of unsuccessful attempts to curtail the leakage, the TVA decommissioned Hales Bar Dam and constructed a new facility, Nickajack Dam, about six miles downstream. Nickajack Dam began operations in late 1967.

Today, all that remains of Hales Bar Dam is the powerhouse on the east bank of the Tennessee River. Most of the interior that once housed generators and turbines for producing electricity is now open space used as a dry boat storage area for Hales Bar Marina.

But the ghostly remnants of the past still linger in the powerhouse and tunnel under the river. One of the original turbines is still in place, and a whirlpool is constantly created in the moving water.

The whirlpool serves as a lingering reminder of the valiant efforts to tame the turbulent Tennessee River. During construction of the dam, some of the land surrounding the river was flooded. According to local legend, a portion of the flooded area was a sacred Cherokee burial ground. Some say the souls buried beneath the river are still making their presence known from the depths of the whirlpool, churning the waters with their restless spirits. A few people have even claimed that they have peered down into the circling waters and could see watery faces of the desperate souls—much like the Cherokee of the legend who was trapped in the spiraling waters of the Suck.

Within the powerhouse the spiral staircase still takes visitors into the dimly lit tunnel that workers and schoolchildren once used to travel from one side of the river to the other. Though a cemetery on a hillside overlooking the structure contains gravesites of many of the workers and their families, some say the spooky tunnel is haunted with the souls of the workers and children who lived here.

One episode of the Travel Channel's series *Ghost Adventures* explored the powerhouse and tunnel. Paranormal investigators recorded eerie noises in the tunnel, sounding much like ghostly voices and children's laughter. Video cameras caught shadowy forms creeping through a balcony in the powerhouse. The cable show also featured local paranormal explorers who insisted they had come into physical contact with the ghostly spirits who continue to haunt the tunnel. Some said they had experienced burning sensations on their chests, scratches on their arms, tugs on shirts, and forces yanking on their hair.

One employee of the Hales Bar Marina and Resort claimed that the ghostly spirits residing in the tunnel gave him the scare of his life. During a heart-stopping moment in the tunnel, a shadow came around the maintenance worker and consumed him with such terror that he passed out.

The Hales Bar Dam and Resort now offers floating cabins for rent, along with pontoon boats for exploring the Tennessee River, giving visitors a front-row seat to the scenic beauty of the area—and the chance to experience the spirits of the past that may linger in the territory that once belonged to the Cherokee.

CHAPTER 8

The Mummy Mystery

History tells us that President Abraham Lincoln was assassinated on the evening of April 14, 1865, in Washington, D.C., as he watched a performance in Ford's Theatre. Actor John Wilkes Booth crept into the president's box, fired a single shot into the back of the president's head, and escaped into the night.

Twelve days after the assassination, Union cavalry tracked Booth and a comrade to a tobacco barn in Virginia. Booth's companion surrendered, but the assassin refused to leave the barn. The soldiers shot Booth in the neck, set fire to the building, and dragged him from the structure. He died a short time later.

But was the man pulled from the barn actually John Wilkes Booth? Could the soldiers have mistakenly caught the wrong person? What really happened to President Lincoln's assassin?

Almost immediately after the announcement of Booth's capture and death, rumors of Booth sightings rippled throughout the nation and spread to foreign shores. Six weeks after Lincoln's murder, one couple claimed that Booth had boarded a ship in Havana, Cuba, and sailed with them to Nassau. In return for the couple's kindness, Booth gave the woman a ring engraved inside with the initials "J.W.B." One newspaper reported that Booth had been spotted in Brazil, and a justice of the peace claimed he ran into Booth in Maryland during the 1870s.

But it was an attorney from Memphis, Tennessee, who claimed to know the real story about the fate of John Wilkes Booth. The attorney, Finis Bates, insisted that Booth had escaped capture, traveled through the South, assumed two different names, and lived into the twentieth century. Moreover, Bates proclaimed that he possessed solid proof of his claim: a mummified corpse of the late John Wilkes Booth.

In 1886 Finis Bates notified the War Department that the real John Wilkes Booth was living in Texas under the name John St. Helen. Bates claimed that the man had made a deathbed confession to him, eventually recovered from his illness, and revealed more details about the Booth family and the events surrounding the assassination.

Though Army officials refused to reopen the case, Bates never forgot what he heard. He spent the rest of his life researching the Lincoln assassination and the man who pulled the trigger on the sixteenth president of the United States.

In 1907 Bates published *The Escape and Suicide of John Wilkes Booth: Or the First True Account of Lincoln's Assassination, Containing a Complete Confession by Booth Many Years After His*

Crime. The attorney's book recounted detailed confessions of the man who proclaimed to be John Wilkes Booth.

As the story goes, Finis Langdon Bates began his legal career in Granbury, Texas. In 1872 the young lawyer encountered a man by the name of John St. Helen who approached him about obtaining a liquor license. Bates immediately noticed that the man's poise, dress, and oratorical skills set him apart from other residents of the Texas town. St. Helen frequently cited passages from *Macbeth,* always attended theatrical performances, and dressed immaculately in stylish fashions. On one occasion, however, Bates noticed that St. Helen panicked when he was called to testify in federal court on behalf of another one of Bates's clients. The eloquent man eventually confessed to Bates that his last name was not actually St. Helen but refused to explain anything more.

One evening in the mid-1870s, Bates was summoned to St. Helen's bedside. Feverish and deathly ill, St. Helen assumed he was dying and asked to speak privately to Bates. When the attorney arrived, St. Helen made an astonishing confession: He was John Wilkes Booth. He handed the lawyer a photo of himself, asking Bates to send it to his brother, the actor Edwin Booth, who would want to know of his death.

St. Helen, however, eventually recovered from his illness. In later conversations with Bates, St. Helen—or Booth—described the murder of Lincoln and his escape in vivid detail. He explained that he had escaped from the Virginia farm only a few hours before the arrival of the Army soldiers. After realizing he had lost some letters and personal identification along his escape route, he sent a man back to the farm to retrieve his belongings. St. Helen suspected that the man had entered the barn and died in his place.

Soon after his recovery St. Helen left the town of Granbury. Several years later Bates also left Texas and moved to Memphis, where he established a law practice. He earned an excellent reputation as a land title attorney, would later serve as assistant district attorney for Shelby County, and would also become the grandfather of the award-winning actress Kathy Bates. But his real interest was the Booth/St. Helen controversy, and he refused to let it die. He constantly researched the mystery, even discovering grains of truth behind many of St. Helen's claims. For instance, long after St. Helen revealed that he, as Booth, had lost his field glasses at the farm, the public release of the official investigative records confirmed that Booth's field glasses had been found in the yard.

Then, in 1903, Bates received some startling news. A house painter by the name of David E. George had committed suicide in the small town of Enid, Oklahoma. On his deathbed he had confessed to several local residents that his real name was John Wilkes Booth.

As soon as he learned of the dying man's confession, Bates immediately thought of his Texas friend. Could David George also be his friend John St. Helen? Bates soon learned that George was often drunk as he sat in his boarding house, reading theatrical journals and quoting Shakespeare. He once lamented to his landlady, "I'm not an ordinary painter. You don't know who I am. I killed the best man that ever lived." Within a short time he swallowed a massive amount of poison and died.

Since George died without leaving a will or money for a funeral, no one in Enid wanted responsibility for disposing of the body of John Wilkes Booth. The townspeople even discussed burning his body in retaliation for his murderous act against their beloved President Lincoln. Town officials, however, decided to preserve George's body in anticipation of the arrival of Washington officials. They were certain someone from Washington would come to their little town to validate George's claims that he was actually John Wilkes Booth.

By the time Bates arrived in Enid, he discovered that the undertaker had embalmed, but not buried, the corpse. Some accounts claim that the undertaker actually mummified the body with arsenic. Others contend that George had poisoned himself with arsenic, and the corpse mummified in combination with the embalming fluid and the hot, dry air of central Oklahoma.

As soon as Bates gazed upon the dead man's face, he immediately recognized him. "My old friend!" he exclaimed. "My old friend John St. Helen!"

Bates paid the embalming bill and requested to take the corpse back with him to Memphis. The transfer was sanctioned by an Oklahoma judge. Since Bates had once served as John St.

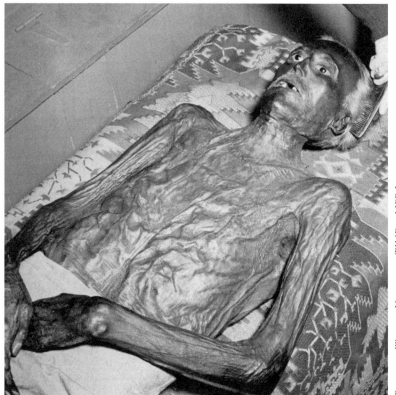

Carnivals displayed this mummy of David E. George—also known as John St. Helen and John Wilkes Booth—during the 1930s.

Helen's attorney, the judge must have assumed that Bates would make sure his former client received a decent burial.

Bates, however, may have believed he could make some money from his strange acquisition. Taking the mummy home with him, he carefully stored it in a crate in his garage while he penned about his experiences with St. Helen and compiled the information into a book of more than three hundred pages.

80

To promote the book's release in 1907, Bates took the mummy with him on book tours and signings. Bates hoped the book and the mummy exhibition would finally convince the Army to reopen the case. Although the book went through several printings, Bates's dream never materialized.

After his death in 1923, however, interest in Bates's theory increased when an article on the subject appeared in the November 1924 issue of *Harper's Magazine.* The author, who had personally examined the mummy in Memphis, concluded that "the evidence against the Enid legend is simply overwhelming." He ended the article by saying, "But what a strange story it is!"

The Booth mummy remained in Memphis for twenty years before Bates's widow sold it to a carnival for one thousand dollars. During the 1930s the mummy became a major attraction at Jay Gould's Million Dollar Spectacle, a carnival traveling the Midwest. For the admission price of twenty-five cents, carnivalgoers could inspect the mummy, which was dressed in khaki shorts and laid out on an Indian blanket. And a sign promised ten thousand dollars to anyone who could prove the mummy was not genuine.

In 1931 Chicago physicians x-rayed the mummy, probably at the request of carnival owners. Amazingly, they found similarities between marks on the mummy and descriptions of Booth's injuries over the years.

Booth had once crushed his right thumb in a curtain gear onstage, and the mummy's right thumb was disjointed. When Booth rushed from the Ford Theatre on the night of Lincoln's

assassination, the spur of his boot became tangled in a flag drap-
ing the balcony, fracturing his leg about six inches above the
ankle. The corpse had a fractured left fibula. Other markings,
such as a scarred eyebrow, also matched physical descriptions of
Booth. Incredibly, the size of the mummy's foot also matched the
size of a boot left behind by Booth during his escape.

Moreover, the X-rays also revealed an object in the mummy's
stomach—a signet ring with the initial "B." Did Booth swallow a
ring during his escape to destroy evidence of his identity?

Though most people considered the X-rays to be a publicity stunt, no one could deny that the corpse was a real human
mummy. But one question remained: Was the mummy truly
John Wilkes Booth?

According to one researcher, Booth may have lived in Tennessee for a short time after Lincoln's assassination. Before his
death in 2002, the late Dr. Arthur Ben Chitty, historiographer
at the University of the South in Sewanee, Tennessee, spent
forty years researching Booth's connections to Tennessee. Chitty
uncovered stories that Booth, using the alias John St. Helen, had
arrived in Tennessee after Lincoln's assassination and married a
woman named Louisa Payne.

Chitty's interviews with local residents revealed that Payne,
a devout Christian, had insisted that St. Helen remarry her under
his given name. Marriage license records from Franklin County,
Tennessee, confirm that a license was issued for "John W. Booth
to Louisa J. Payne on February 24, 1872." C. C. Rose, justice of

the peace, stated, "I solemnized the rite of matrimony between the within named parties on the twenty-fifth day of February 1872." The license was signed by "Jno. W. Booth."

Another local resident in Sewanee told Chitty that one of his childhood friends was McCager Payne, the son of Louisa Payne and the stepson of her husband, John St. Helen.

In 1926 the *Clarksville Leaf-Chronicle* published an interview with McCager Payne. During the interview, Payne revealed he had overheard his stepfather tell his mother about "knots on his left leg" and admit that he was Booth. Once his stepfather realized the boy had overheard the conversation, he warned, "If you ever tell what you heard me say, I'll rip your throat from ear to ear."

Several years later, according to McCager Payne, St. Helen moved west to Texas and lost touch with his family. Other archival records show that St. Helen took his wife and stepson to Memphis, then left them and went to Texas. Louisa Payne and her son returned to Sewanee. After St. Helen's disappearance, Louisa gave birth to their daughter, Laura Ida Elizabeth Booth.

Nate Orlowek, a Booth researcher who collaborated with Dr. Chitty to reexamine the story of Booth's death, discovered that Booth's descendents were told by older family members that Booth had escaped and lived for years under aliases. One niece claimed that Booth had secretly met with her mother for a year after the assassination and had lived for another thirty-seven years.

At the close of the twentieth century, Booth's descendents were questioning the validity of the body buried in their family plot in Green Mount Cemetery in Baltimore. According to historical accounts, several Union soldiers who were acquainted with John Wilkes Booth had identified his body after the Virginia barn was set ablaze. The corpse was transported to Washington for autopsy and placed inside a warehouse storage area. In 1869 the War Department turned over the body to the Booth family. Members of the family and dental records confirmed the identity of the body before burial in Baltimore.

Did Bates's book convince the Booth family and others that the wrong man is buried in Booth's grave? Is the comparison between Booth's physical appearance and the mummified corpse too similar to ignore? Or are the stories of John St. Helen and David George only two pieces of the unsolved mystery?

Adding to the mystery is the possibility that the man captured in the Virginia barn after Lincoln's assassination may have borne little resemblance to the dark-haired Booth. Some soldiers described the man as a redhead with freckles. According to some reports, David Herold, Booth's comrade who was nabbed by Union soldiers at the Virginia farm, was puzzled by the man's identity. Herold supposedly asked his captors, "Who was that man in the barn with me? He told me his name was Boyd."

Though hundreds of people in Washington, D.C., knew Booth, some say that no close friends were asked to identify his remains. Instead, the Army relied on a few military men who had seen Booth onstage, along with the proprietor of a Washington hotel where Booth had lodged. Did the government realize it had the wrong man? Was the rush to identify Booth and conduct an autopsy and burial part of a government cover-up?

Another account reveals testimony from Booth's personal physician. As he examined the body, he stated, "My surprise was so great that I at once said . . . 'There is no resemblance in that corpse to Booth, nor can I believe it to be that of him.' Never in a human being had a greater change taken place."

Other Booth historians claim that several close acquaintances identified Booth's body before burial and noted that "JWB" was tattooed on the hand of the dead man, as it had been on John Wilkes Booth. And the body, just like the mummy, was scarred in all the right places. The undershirt on the body was pinned together with an engraved pin, a gift to Booth from a friend. The clerk at Washington's National Hotel, where Booth was a frequent guest and had stayed the night before the assassination, confidently identified the body as Booth's, as well as the clothes on the corpse.

In 1995 Booth's family requested that the body be exhumed for studies to determine if the corpse was actually John Wilkes Booth. Though the state supported their efforts, the cemetery took the case to court, and a judge ruled that the "escape/cover up theory" was "less than convincing" and prohibited disinterring the body.

But one more option may confirm or disprove that the body in the Maryland cemetery is Booth's. Before burial a few vertebrae were removed from Booth's body. Today, the Armed Forces

Institute for Pathology possesses those remains. If the institute would permit scientists to compare the family's DNA to the vertebra removed from Booth's body, the mystery may be solved.

Could the mummy provide DNA evidence as well? With their sophisticated equipment, scientists could analyze physical characteristics of Booth to determine if they matched the mummy. Maybe so, but no one can locate it. The mummy enjoyed a long career as a carnival sideshow attraction during Bates's lifetime and after his death. In 1942 the mummy officially belonged to John Harkin, the tattooed man in the Hagenbeck-Wallace Circus. The last documented sighting of the mummy occurred during the early 1960s in Philadelphia. One man claimed he saw the mummy in the mid-1970s at a Pennsylvania carnival, complete with the X-rays made in Chicago.

Though the body of David George, or John St. Helen, or John Wilkes Booth—or perhaps all three—has vanished from public eye, some people suspect it may be in the hands of a private collector. Still, the Regional Forensic Center in Memphis and the Smithsonian Institution in Washington, D.C., have expressed interest in examining the mummy.

Many people may think Finis Bates was eccentric and odd for housing the body of a mummy in his garage and persistently pursuing his theory of John Wilkes Booth's escape. Yet others contend the investigation by a young attorney from Memphis may have been on the right track. Perhaps one day the case of the mysterious mummy will be solved.

CHAPTER 9

Cherokee Myths and Legends

L ong before the arrival of the white man, Cherokee Indians lived, worked, and played in the area now known as Tennessee. Cherokee storytellers passed down oral histories and stories to their people, and the tales were retold, generation after generation. Many of the tribe's tales carried mythical tones involving animals, nature, creation, and the supernatural.

Several Cherokee legends also told of star-crossed lovers. One of the most well-known tales centers on Sautee, a young brave from an enemy tribe, and Nacoochee, the daughter of the chief of the Cherokees.

Sautee's love for the beautiful Nacoochee blossomed from the day he first saw the Cherokee princess, whose name translates as "Evening Star." Though he realized the rivalry between their tribes strictly forbade him to court Nacoochee, Sautee was determined to overcome the obstacles and win her heart.

Nacoochee, too, knew her father would never consent to the union. If she were to marry Sautee, she would have to sacrifice everything dear to her, including her home, her friends, and her family. Still, Nacoochee's love for Sautee grew so powerful that she could not resist the temptation to elope with her lover.

Sautee's tribe adamantly opposed the marriage and refused to allow Nacoochee to reside with them. Without the support of their warring families, Sautee and Nacoochee set up their own home in a cave on the side of Lookout Mountain, Tennessee.

Native plants, trees, and shrubs hid the entrance of the cave from view, concealing their hideout from the rest of the world. Sautee's marksmanship skills with a bow and arrow provided plenty of game for food, while a nearby spring furnished water for the pair.

But as the young couple began their lives together, Evening Star's father vowed to seek revenge against Sautee. Enlisting the help of young Cherokee braves, the father sent out a search party to find and capture Sautee. The braves soon located Sautee and brought him to Evening Star's father.

The Cherokee chief sentenced Sautee to death and ordered his braves to throw his daughter's lover from a high cliff on the side of Lookout Mountain. The entire tribe gathered on top of the mountain to witness the murder. Nacoochee was also present, forced to watch the preparations for her beloved Sautee's demise.

Sautee did not flinch as he prepared to meet his fate. The proud Indian stood straight and tall and sang the song of death with a clear, strong voice. The sounds of his voice were still echoing through the mountains and valleys when two strong braves raised him high in the air and hurled him over the cliff.

While the tribe focused on the tragedy, Nacoochee seized the opportunity to step to the edge of the cliff. "Sautee! Sautee!" were the last words from her lips as she leaped from the ledge and plummeted some one hundred feet to join her beloved Sautee in death. Nacoochee's grief-stricken father buried the lovers side by side in the valley of their death. Today, visitors to Rock City Gardens atop Lookout Mountain can step onto the same ledge that witnessed the tragic deaths of the legendary lovers. This cliff is now known as Lover's Leap.

This illustration of Lover's Leap is from an undated postcard.

Another romantic myth of the Cherokees symbolizes the enduring power of love. In 1780 the Cherokees found a British officer who had been severely wounded in the Battle of King's Mountain and took him to their village to recuperate from his injuries. Nocatula, daughter of Chief Attakullakulla, nursed the soldier back to health. Along the way, the Indian princess and former British soldier fell deeply in love. The Cherokee chief blessed the union and gave the name "Conestoga" to the man, a Cherokee word meaning "oak."

But Mocking Crow, one of Nocatula's former suitors, flew into a jealous rage, ambushed Conestoga, and murdered him. Nocatula immediately rushed to Conestoga's side, but it was too late. Devastated by the death of her lover, she pulled out the bloody knife—the murder weapon—from his body. Then she thrust the knife into her own heart.

Chief Attakullakulla buried the bodies side by side at the site of their deaths. In Conestoga's right hand the Chief placed an acorn. In his daughter's right hand, he placed a hackberry seed. The following year the graves of the two lovers held sprouts of an oak tree and a hackberry tree. As the years passed, the trunks of the two trees blended together and the branches intertwined.

The pair of trees stood together for decades on the grounds of the former Athens Female College, now known as Tennessee Wesleyan College, in Athens, Tennessee. In 1945 the hackberry tree died and was removed from the site. Like the legendary lovers, Conestoga and Nocatula, the oak tree failed to survive

FROM *THE ANTIQUITIES OF TENNESSEE AND THE ADJACENT STATES* BY GATES PHILLIPS THRUSTON, 1897

Animals and insects were often the subjects of Cherokee myths, as illustrated by this Cherokee shell gorget featuring a spider design.

without its mate. Within five years the mighty oak withered and died.

A historical marker was erected on the site in 1957, recounting the legend of the lovers, and two new trees were planted where the original trees once stood.

In 1887 and 1888 James Mooney, a representative of the US Bureau of American Ethnology, convinced many prominent Cherokee storytellers to tell him about the most popular Cherokee myths and explain the cultural meanings of the tales. He published the myths in his 1902 book, *Myths of the Cherokees*.

Mooney revealed that many Cherokee fables used symbols of nature as characters to emphasize a universal truth. The myth "The Bride from the South" suggests that the union of two cultures may be difficult to sustain over time.

As the story goes, the North traveled far and wide until he found the woman he wanted to marry, known as the daughter of the South. But her parents objected to the match, claiming that North had brought cold weather with him, and they might freeze to death if he stayed.

After North pleaded with the parents to let him take their daughter back to his own country, they finally consented to his proposal. The couple soon married and returned to North's country. To the young bride's surprise, she discovered that everyone lived in ice houses.

When the sun rose the following day, the houses began to leak. As the sun climbed higher into the sky, the temperatures increased so much that the houses began to melt. Finally, the people told North he must send his wife home or the entire settlement would melt.

North, however, loved his wife and refused to send her away. But as the sun grew hotter and hotter, the people grew more insistent. His wife was a native of the South, they claimed, and her warm nature was unfit for the North. In the end North conceded to the people's demands and sent his wife home to her parents.

According to Mooney, many Cherokee myths involved stories about birds and animals, such as the humorous myth of

"The Race between the Crane and the Hummingbird." In this story a pretty woman was pursued by both the hummingbird and the crane. Though she favored the handsome hummingbird, the awkward crane persistently courted her. To get rid of the crane, the young woman said he must challenge the hummingbird to a race. Then she would marry the winner.

The woman was certain the hummingbird would win, since he was as fast as lightning, while the crane was big and slow. But she didn't realize the crane could fly throughout the darkness of night.

The two birds agreed to start the race from the woman's house and fly around the world. The winner would be the lucky one to marry the woman.

As the race began, the hummingbird darted off like an arrow and disappeared from sight. He flew all day, and by the time he stopped to rest for the night, he knew he must be far ahead of the crane.

But the crane flew steadily all day and night, passing the hummingbird shortly after midnight. Around daylight, he stopped by a creek to rest.

The hummingbird awakened the next morning and started his flight again, thinking he could easily win the race. But when he reached the creek, he was surprised to see the crane using his long bill to spear tadpoles for breakfast. Wondering how the crane could have passed him, he swiftly flew by and disappeared from sight again.

When the crane finished his breakfast, he started the next leg of his journey. As dusk approached, he continued his trek. This time, before midnight he passed the hummingbird asleep on a limb. By the time the hummingbird caught up with him the next morning, he had finished his breakfast.

The next day the crane gained more distance. On the fourth day the hummingbird passed by as the crane was spearing tadpoles for dinner. By the seventh day the crane was ahead of the hummingbird by an entire night's travel time.

Early in the morning on the seventh day of the race, the crane had a leisurely breakfast, spruced himself up at the creek, and crossed the finish line at the woman's house. By the time the hummingbird arrived late in the afternoon, he was dismayed to find he had lost the race.

But the crane was dismayed as well when he discovered he did not reap the rewards of winning the race. The woman declared she would never have such an ugly fellow as the crane for a husband, and she decided not to marry anyone at all.

Other Cherokee myths bear strong similarities to modern fairy tales, such as the story about an ugly bullfrog that turns into a handsome prince after being kissed by a beautiful maiden. However, as Mooney's book reveals, the Cherokee adaptation of "The Bullfrog Lover" has some unexpected twists and turns in the plot.

In this myth a mother was so opposed to the young man who was courting her daughter that she would not allow him to come near the house. One evening the young man hid near a spring and waited until the old woman arrived to get some water. The enterprising suitor had made a trumpet from the handle of a gourd. While the woman dipped up the water, he put the trumpet to his lips. With his voice sounding like the grumble of a bullfrog, he warned, "The faultfinder will die."

Frightened, the woman dropped the dipper and dashed back to the house. She told her family about the incident, claiming a witch bullfrog had spoken to her. Everyone agreed that she was being warned to stop interfering with her daughter's affairs. The woman decided they were right and consented to the young man courting her daughter.

In another version of this tale, a young girl went to the spring for water every day. Each time she heard a voice singing, "A bullfrog will marry you! A bullfrog will marry you!" One day she saw a bullfrog sitting on a stone by the spring. Suddenly, the bullfrog turned into a young man, and he asked her to marry him. She immediately consented, and they went to her home so he could meet her family.

But the girl's family took one look at the man and disliked the strange bullfrog appearance about his face. They eventually persuaded her to send him away.

The next time her family went down to the spring, they heard a voice saying, "Your daughter will die! Your daughter will die!" Unfortunately, the prediction came true, and the daughter died soon after.

In yet a third version of this mythical tale, the lover was a tadpole. Though he took on a human form, his mouth remained in the shape of a tadpole's mouth. To conceal his identity, he refused to eat with the family. Instead, he stood with his back to the table, twisting his face, and pretending he had a toothache. His wife finally turned him around to face the firelight and exposed the tadpole mouth. All of the family ridiculed him so much that he left the house and never returned.

Owls and other nocturnal birds also play major roles in Cherokee myths. According to Mooney, the Cherokees believe owls are actually ghosts or disguised witches, and the hoot of the owl signifies the sound of an evil omen. The Cherokee myth "The Owl Gets Married" exemplifies this belief.

In this myth a widow warned her only daughter that she must choose a good hunter for a husband. When a suitor came to call on the girl, the widow said only a good hunter could have her daughter. The suitor claimed he was a suitable match, so the mother advised her daughter to take him.

So the courtship was arranged, and the man lived with the girl. The next morning he said he was getting ready to go hunting. Before leaving he changed his mind and decided to go fishing. That evening he brought home only three small fish, claiming he had no luck that day but would have better luck tomorrow.

The next evening he came home with only two spring lizards and the same excuse. The following night he returned with a few scraps of deer that he had found, explaining that some hunters had left behind the scraps after cutting up a deer.

By this time the old woman was suspicious. So next morning she told her daughter to secretly follow him through the woods and see what he was doing. The girl obediently followed her husband, keeping him in sight until he came to the river. Then she saw him change into a hooting owl and fly over to a pile of driftwood.

Surprised and angry, the girl watched the owl swoop down, scoop up some sand in his claws, and pick out a crawfish. Then he flew across to the bank, took the form of a man again, and started home with the crawfish. His wife scurried through the woods and returned home before he arrived.

When he entered the house with the crawfish, she asked, "Where are all the fish you caught?" He explained that an owl had frightened them away. "I think you are the owl," she said and threw him out of the house.

The owl went into the woods and pined away with grief and love.

Whether you believe in spirits taking the form of nature, animals turning into human forms, or lovers unwilling to live without their mates by their side, the Cherokee who once lived in Tennessee weaved fascinating myths that continue to play a major role in the state's heritage and culture.

CHAPTER 10

The Mystery of the Old Stone Fort

With a fleeting glance, you see nothing more than mounds of earthen embankments surrounding a large, flat field in Coffee County, Tennessee. But the Old Stone Fort State Archaeological Park in Manchester is one of the most mysterious places in the Volunteer State.

The unusual site, shaped somewhat like a pear, consists of earthen walls made from stacked stones and piles of rock and covered by dirt from the beds of the rivers and the immediate vicinity. These embankments, about four to six feet in height, form an enclosure around a plateau that is surrounded by two rivers and steep cliffs. Combined with the surrounding cliffs and rivers, the mounds and walls form an enclosure that measures more than one mile long.

But no one knows for certain who built it or when or why it was constructed.

When Tennessee's first white settlers stumbled upon the fifty-acre tract in the late 1700s, they could find no evidence of who had erected the enclosure or why it had been constructed. Moreover, no one who lived in the region could offer any explanations. "The oldest Indians, of the first settlement of Tennessee, stated that they had heard their fathers speak of it, but their earliest traditions had not traced its origin," stated William Donnison, a Nashville attorney, in 1818. His statements appeared in the *Columbian Centinal,* a Boston newspaper published twice a week, in July of the following year.

One of the first recorded references to the site occurred in 1794. Soldiers invading Cherokee towns camped within its walls as they traveled along an old Indian trail. The nearby town of Manchester, founded in 1836, was known for many years as Old Stone Fort. Though early maps labeled the area as the "Old Stone Fort," most of the first settlers were skeptical that the enclosure had been built by Native Americans. After all, they were accustomed to fences made of pointed logs that typically surrounded Indian villages, not walls made of earth and stone.

Still, the natural configuration of the terrain provided the perfect setting for a fortification. The two rivers surrounding the Old Stone Fort, the Big Duck and Little Duck, come close together, then spread apart, descend, and merge. The area between the rivers makes a large, flat plateau, which is enclosed by the earthen walls and cliffs. The walls go almost all the way around the enclosure, except for a few places where sheer cliffs are below the bluff. The cliffs made attacks from intruders practically impossible.

The enclosure also includes a complex entranceway, originally thirty-two feet wide, consisting of a moatlike ditch, mounds on either side of the entrance, and interior walls. The entrance mounds, about three feet higher than the main walls and strengthened with additional stonework, could have easily served as points for lookouts. With the design of the entrance, early historians believed explorers, possibly Welsh or Norse, or the Spanish troops led by Hernando de Soto, must have built the area to serve as a fort for defense.

In fact, the *Jackson Pioneer* newspaper in Jackson, Tennessee, published a theory about "Buccaneers of Seville" as the builders of the Old Stone Fort. In 1823 the newspaper stated that a package of charts, journals, and papers had been discovered in an old building in Seville, Spain. The old documents revealed that a Spanish vessel had shipwrecked in Florida during the early sixteenth century. The pirates moved northward, built the Old Stone Fort for protection from Indians, and remained there for about twenty years. Later inquiries to Seville officials, however, could not confirm any documentation about the Spanish pirates from Seville.

During the 1560s explorer Juan Pardo established the first Spanish settlement in the interior of North Carolina. Twenty years earlier Hernando de Soto explored the southeastern United States. Could either of these men have built the Old Stone Fort? No record exists of Pardo being in the area now known as Middle Tennessee. One historian claims that de Soto built a similar structure, Fort Mountain, in nearby Murray County, Georgia, in 1540. But other researchers contend that de Soto, constantly in search of gold and riches, had neither the time nor desire to build forts.

French explorer Robert Cavelier de la Salle described the Old Stone Fort in a report of his exploration of the Mississippi Valley in 1692. He stated it was occupied at the time by the Yuchi Indians, sometimes known as the Chisca tribe. Some historians say the Yuchi Indians could possibly have built the fort, since the tribe settled in the eastern portion of Tennessee around 1400. In fact, de Soto learned of a rich province called Chisca in 1540 and sent scouts to investigate the rumor that gold and copper were being mined in the province. But the scouts returned from the journey and reported that the mountainous terrain was far too difficult for the group to explore.

Still, other historians contend that the Cherokee Indians of the eastern part of the state, or the Chickasaws of the western part, possibly had the skills and knowledge to build the Old Stone Fort. Some speculated that the pear-shaped area of the site indicated that Native Americans had built the area in effigy form to resemble a turtle or bear. Evidence to support the building of the fort by either tribe, however, has yet to surface.

One clue regarding the age of the fort came to light in 1819 when the owner of the property cut down a white oak tree that was growing on top of one of the earth-covered walls. The man counted 357 rings in the sliced tree trunk. If each ring accounted

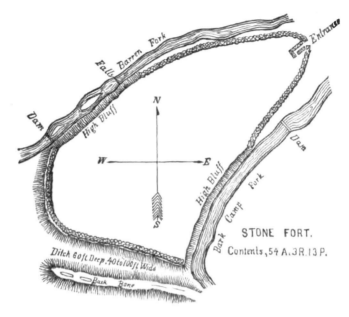

FROM *THE ANTIQUITIES OF TENNESSEE AND THE ADJACENT STATES* BY GATES PHILLIPS THRUSTON, 1897

Survey of Old Stone Fort by Joseph Jones, 1876.

for one year of growth, the tree was at least 357 years old. And that means the tree sprouted around 1462, some thirty years before Columbus first saw America and long before the arrival of the Spanish.

In 1876 Joseph Jones with the Smithsonian Institution investigated the fort. Jones personally explored the site and hired a resident of Manchester to survey and plat the area. Historians believe Jones's survey was much more accurate than verbal reports of earlier years, although he could not conclude who built the site or when it was constructed. Like others, Jones suspected that the site had been built for defense purposes.

Yet Jones found nothing to indicate the grounds had been occupied by anyone other than soldiers during the Civil War. His written report revealed that "the fort had been used by soldiers during a portion of the recent war (1861–65) for a camping ground" and that "fragments of iron utensils and of copper are occasionally found, also lead bullets, but these are clearly of modern date."

Another fifty years passed before a second survey was conducted. In 1928 Tennessee state archaeologist P. E. Cox devoted two weeks to excavating various portions of the fort's walls and interior area. But Cox, like Jones and others, could not solve the riddle of its age, function, or builders.

In the 1950s a new, more convincing theory surfaced about the Old Stone Fort in the book *Who Discovered America?* The author, Zella Armstrong, Chattanooga amateur archaeologist and history buff, speculated the site had been built by Welshmen who arrived in North America during the twelfth century.

Welsh history has documented that Prince Madoc of Wales landed in the area of the Gulf Coast around 1170. In fact, Madoc made a total of three successful trips to the region. At some point he convinced his family and friends in Wales that they should travel with him to the quiet, peaceful land that he had discovered, and start a new chapter of their lives in this beautiful place.

Armstrong speculated that Madoc left a group of people— probably around three hundred to five hundred men, women, and children—near the mouth of the Alabama River in Mobile

Bay. Intending to settle in the region, they traveled through the Alabama River valleys and made their way to Tennessee. Along the way, they came into contact with Indians who may have been less than friendly. Since gunpowder and firearms were not yet available, the Welsh settlers could have constructed the Old Stone Fort to protect themselves from Indian attacks.

The walled enclosure at the Old Stone Fort resembled similar structures in Wales, Armstrong noted. Moreover, the name of the river that flows near Mobile—the Dog River—could have been derived from the prince's name in old Welsh: *Madog ap Owain Gwynedd.*

Adding to the puzzle is the fact that early English explorers noticed certain Indian languages contained guttural sounds very similar to Welsh speech patterns. Moreover, numerous accounts have been recorded of Indians throughout the area of present-day Tennessee, Kentucky, and Missouri who had unmistakable characteristics of white Anglo-Saxons and knowledge of the Welsh language. Could these so-called "Welsh Indians" have been descendents of Madoc's group who intermarried with Native American tribes? And could they have been the builders of the Old Stone Fort?

In the 1960s scientists unearthed evidence that Europeans had been present in North America nearly five hundred years before Christopher Columbus. When ruins of a Norse village dating to around AD 1000 were discovered in Newfoundland, Armstrong's theory of Welsh settlers in America sounded much more feasible.

In fact, some people thought the Old Stone Fort had been built by Vikings. When two huge masses of molten metal were found within four miles of the Old Stone Fort, archaeologists considered the possibility that Vikings had been present in the area and may have built the site. After all, iron slag and molten metal had been discovered in North America where the Vikings had supposedly lived. Could the Vikings or their descendents have worked their way inland from coastal areas and constructed a fortress in Middle Tennessee?

The Smithsonian Institution examined samples of the slag and concluded they were made by man, possibly in an attempt to produce iron. Yet an analysis by a metallurgist revealed that one mass was more than 90 percent pure iron, indicating that the material could have been formed in the ground as a natural element.

The mystery of the age of the fort lingered until 1966 when the state of Tennessee purchased four hundred acres of land, which included the site of the Old Stone Fort, for developing a state park. The state immediately engaged the University of Tennessee's anthropology department to conduct an extensive archaeological dig to determine the age, function, and builders of the Old Stone Fort.

Armed with new technology and archaeological tools, researchers recovered charcoal remains from several points in the Old Stone Fort for analysis. With radiocarbon testing, they learned the Old Stone Fort was built over a period of five hundred years by two groups of people. The entrance ditch, they estimated, was constructed around AD 80, while the walls were completed about AD 550. This prehistoric era of two thousand years ago was known as the Middle Woodland period.

Archaeologists also noted that the Old Stone Fort was constructed about the same time as similar hilltop enclosure sites, including Fort Ancient in Warren County, Ohio, built by the Hopewells. This group of Native Americans was known for building mounds. The Pinson Mounds, located in the area now known as West Tennessee, were also built during this era.

Several years after the excavation of the Old Stone Fort, University of Tennessee archaeologists discovered small village sites once inhabited by the McFarland and Owl Hollow people near the Old Stone Fort. Extensive radiocarbon dating of these early farming and pottery-making communities revealed that the McFarland people resided in the area between 200 BC and AD 200. The Owl Hollow people followed the McFarlands, living in the region between AD 200 and 600.

With these new revelations, researchers concluded that the Hopewells came into contact with the McFarland and Owl Hollow cultures and may have taught them the necessary skills to construct the Old Stone Fort. The McFarland culture apparently began building the Old Stone Fort in the first century AD, and the Owl Hollow people completed the structure nearly five hundred years later.

Charles H. Faulkner, one of the University of Tennessee researchers who excavated the site in 1966, pointed out that very few artifacts or human remains had been found inside the Old Stone Fort. The absence of human remains implies that the site was never used as burial or sacrificial grounds, and the lack of artifacts suggests that the Old Stone Fort had never been occupied by any culture.

In Faulkner's book *The Old Stone Fort: Exploring an Archaeological Mystery,* the author argued that the walls were much too low to have been used for defense, and the interior of the enclosure was far too large for only a handful of warriors to defend. The dimensions of the site, he assessed, were not substantial enough to serve as a functioning fort.

If the Old Stone Fort was not used for burial, sacrificial, or defense purposes, why was it built? Faulkner suggested the site was built as a ceremonial gathering place. The area may have been designated as a sacred space, and the walls may have symbolically warned outsiders not to enter if they didn't belong to the group. Another archaeologist suggested that it was built as both a sacred space and a defensive site to ward off evil spirits.

The most recent hypothesis is that the Old Stone Fort was used as some kind of celestial observatory. Ancient societies often reenacted creation myths during the time of the summer solstice. And at the narrow neck of land between the two rivers, a set of parallel mound walls point toward the position of the sun at summer solstice sunrise.

Today, the Old Stone Fort is the largest and most complex hilltop enclosure in the southeastern portion of the United

States. The site is now a state archaeological park with an interpretive museum, picnic areas, campgrounds, and playgrounds. Along with the earthen enclosures, the site holds the remains of a stagecoach road, several paper mills, and an area used for making gunpowder by Confederate soldiers.

Still, the mystery of the fort's use remains puzzling to researchers. If the Old Stone Fort was a sacred space, what type of ceremonies did it hold? The answers remain unclear, and the Old Stone Fort may never reveal the secrets that it has hidden within its grounds for centuries.

CHAPTER 11

The Delta Queen's *Mary Greene*

"Pssst."

Startled by the hissing sound in his ear and the wisp of a breath on his neck, Mike Williams jolted awake and sat up straight in his cabin berth.

Alone on the historic *Delta Queen* steamboat, Williams could not imagine who had intruded his cabin in the middle of the night. It was 1984, and the magnificent boat was in winter dry dock for maintenance and repairs. Williams was absolutely certain that everything was locked up tight. Or was it?

Williams grabbed a flashlight and hurled open the door to his cabin. Finding no one in the hallway, he proceeded down the hall to make certain the doors to all eighty passenger cabins were locked. As the caretaker of the *Delta Queen,* Williams knew every inch of the old vessel from stem to stern.

One by one, he tested the locks to each of the passenger cabins. But as he twisted the door knob to Cabin 109, the door opened easily. The hazy glow of the flashlight revealed nothing more than a neatly made bed in the small cabin. "I should have known," Williams grumbled to himself. "You're up to your old tricks, Ma Greene."

He turned on his heel to leave. But as he ambled down the hallway, the distinctive sound of a door slamming stopped him cold. Following the direction of the noise, he headed toward the lower engine room. To his astonishment, he discovered water gushing into the room from a hole in a rusty pipe. The hole was large enough to sink the vessel.

Williams quickly repaired the leak and proceeded back to his room. Now everything was perfectly clear. Williams knew exactly who had awakened him from a sound sleep and directed his attention to a slamming door near the engine room. The well-meaning culprit, who lived and died in Cabin 109 of the *Delta Queen,* was none other than Captain Mary Greene.

Born in 1869, Mary Becker met the love of her life, Gordon C. Greene, during their high school years in Newport, Ohio. She and Captain Greene married in 1890, the same year that he established Greene Line Steamers. Instead of setting up house in a traditional frame structure like most brides of the day, Mary set up housekeeping on her husband's Cincinnati packet boat, the *H. K. Bedford.* Packet boats were small paddle wheelers that carried farm produce, livestock, freight, and passengers over the rivers.

Standing by her husband's side and observing his skills in the pilot house, Mary quickly learned the skills of navigation.

Earning her pilot's license around 1896 or 1897, she became one of the first—if not the first—women to legally operate a riverboat.

Mary soon took command of the *Argand,* which operated at a good profit, partially due to her feminine touch at the wheel. Customers said they liked the "lady captain's" dependability and refinement.

The Greenes eventually expanded their fleet to include a dozen packet boats. Though Mary and her husband were devoted to their lives on the river, the couple embraced parenthood and raised three sons aboard their vessels. In fact, son Tom was born on a riverboat that was stuck in an ice jam.

Gordon Greene died unexpectedly in 1927. Sons Tom and Chris joined their mother in operating the business, and the threesome decided to focus on transporting passengers instead of freight over the rivers. The *Gordon C. Greene* was soon operating at full capacity, taking passengers on trips over the Ohio, Tennessee, Cumberland, and Mississippi Rivers. Captain Mary, who had been piloting boats for thirty years, served not only as the master pilot, but also as hostess.

In 1927, the same year of Gordon Greene's death, two other passenger boats were launched in California with much fanfare. The *Delta Queen* and its sister ship, the *Delta King,* had taken three years to build at a cost of nearly one million dollars each. The two ships were not only beautiful but immensely popular, as they shuttled between San Francisco and Sacramento. Three

The stately *Delta Queen* is reportedly still home to former Captain Mary Green.

decks provided wraparound promenades. Passengers enjoyed the affordable fares, ranging from fifty cents for a berth on the lower deck to five dollars for a cabin with a double bed and private bath on the top deck. Dinners aboard the vessels cost between fifty cents and one dollar. Motorists could even drive aboard the boat and park their cars on the freight deck, much like a ferryboat.

During World War II the *Delta Queen* was drafted into service, transporting troops between ships anchored in the San Francisco Bay area and facilities onshore. Painted battleship gray, the *Queen* often served as a floating barracks. It even experienced a day of combat when some prisoners on Alcatraz rioted and armed riflemen aboard the *Delta Queen* circled the island, firing grenades at the cell blocks until the rioters surrendered.

After the war the US Maritime Commission put the *Delta King* and *Delta Queen* up for auction. With the success of transporting passengers on riverboat cruises on the *Gordon C. Greene,* Captain Tom Greene decided to invest in a second passenger vessel to add to the Greene Line's inland riverboat fleet. Casting a winning bid of $46,250, Captain Greene not only saved the *Delta Queen* from the scrapyard but purchased the boat for a fraction of its original cost of nearly one million dollars in 1927.

In 1947 Captain Tom prepared to transport the *Delta Queen* from San Francisco to Cincinnati. Since the flat-bottom boat would have to be towed through the open seas to the Panama Canal, then up to the Mississippi and Ohio Rivers, shipyard workers boarded it up with lumber and special reinforcements for towing.

News of the *Delta Queen*'s departure from San Francisco on April 17, 1947, made headlines around the world. Newspapers provided daily updates of its journey as the *Delta Queen* passed through the Panama Canal—the first for a river steamboat—and safely arrived at New Orleans on May 21.

The *Delta Queen* traveled by its own steam along the Mississippi River and up the Ohio River to the Greene Line headquarters in Cincinnati, traveling a total of more than thirteen hundred miles on the two rivers. Large crowds flocked to the riverbanks to watch the riverboat along its journey.

During a six-month overhaul at a cost of $750,000, the *Delta Queen* was transformed into a new riverboat, both mechanically and physically. Captain Greene even added a steam calliope to cheerfully announce the steamboat's arrival with spirited tunes and sounds—over the protests of his mother, who thought the loud whistles would be too noisy for those living near the river.

The refurbished *Delta Queen* made its debut on June 30, 1948, on a round-trip from Cincinnati to Cairo, Illinois. At the helm of the 265-foot boat was none other than Captain Mary Green, sharp and alert at age seventy-nine.

Although Captain Mary still navigated the river on her own, her primary role on the *Delta Queen* soon encompassed the duties of hostess. She welcomed guests onboard the boat as if welcoming guests into her home—and, of course, her own home was the majestic *Delta Queen*.

Though Captain Mary reportedly once toasted her son at a captain's dinner, she prohibited the sale of liquor on any of her boats, including the *Delta Queen*. One of Mary's descendents claimed that she banned liquor on the boat because she did not want anyone at her Baptist church to associate her with dealing in spirits, especially after the Prohibition years.

After more than fifty years as a riverboat captain, Mary Greene died in her private cabin on the *Delta Queen* in 1949 at age eighty. The following year Tom Greene suffered a heart attack at age forty-six, collapsing as he operated the wheel of the *Delta Queen*.

A few years after the deaths of Mary and her son, a saloon was added to the *Delta Queen*. On the first day of opening its new Mark Twain Bar in 1953, the boat was preparing to launch from its home port of Cincinnati and head to New Orleans for a Mardi Gras cruise. As the bartender stocked liquor into the shelves, passengers were getting ready to board the ship.

At that moment a barge barreled down the river, lost its steering, and slammed into the *Delta Queen*. The impact completely splintered the bar. The name of the barge responsible for the accident was the *Captain Mary B.* Ironically, Mary Greene's maiden name was Becker.

With Captain Mary's dislike for liquor onboard her vessels, was it mere coincidence that the *Captain Mary B.* destroyed the *Delta Queen*'s new bar? Or was Mary's spirit responsible for letting everyone know that she would not tolerate the sale of liquor onboard? Most people familiar with the *Delta Queen* thought that the incident was no accident—it was Mary's spirit making her wishes known.

The damages to the bar area were eventually repaired, and the Mark Twain Bar reopened without incident. In the following years the *Delta Queen* went through several owners, but it always continued to thrill passengers as it took them down the Mississippi, Ohio, and Tennessee Rivers to the Gulf of Mexico.

But in 1965 an incident involving another cruise ship— one that was also built in 1927—threatened the future of the *Delta Queen*. Ninety people lost their lives when the cruise ship

Yarmouth Castle burned as it traveled from Miami to the Bahamas. Like the *Delta Queen,* the *Yarmouth Castle* was an older wooden ship that many considered to be a fire hazard.

The following year the US Congress passed the first Safety of Life at Sea law, upgrading safety regulations that wooden structures like the *Delta Queen* could never hope to meet. A national campaign protesting the new law promoted the fact that riverboats could implement many fire prevention measures. And the boats were never far from the riverbanks, unlike ships on the open sea.

In late 1970 the *Delta Queen* was granted an exemption from the law. Several congressional extensions and renewals kept the *Queen* steaming down the river until 2008. At that time the legislation was not renewed, and the *Delta Queen* was prohibited from operating as a cruising riverboat.

Throughout the years the *Delta Queen* had carried more than a half million passengers over two million miles of water, including such esteemed travelers as US Presidents Jimmy Carter and Harry Truman and Great Britain's Princess Margaret. The paddleboat was named a National Historic Landmark in 1989.

Today the *Delta Queen* is permanently moored as a stationary hotel on the Tennessee River in Chattanooga, welcoming diners and overnight guests. Visitors still board on the gangway, white rocking chairs are still on the deck, the same china is used for meals, the original grand staircase leads up to the Texas Lounge, and the paddle wheel is still painted a bright red. Sister ship the *Delta King* has operated as a hotel and restaurant in Sacramento since 1989.

Through the *Delta Queen's* transitions over the years, many believe Mary's spirit remains onboard, protecting her beloved riverboat. Some accounts describe a matronly woman walking the ship, sometimes wearing a green robe. Crew members have reported seeing a ghostly apparition of a short, older woman late at night, strolling on the deck as if making her rounds to make sure everything is in order for passengers.

One musician described catching a glimpse of a woman in a 1930s dress from the corner of her eye. But each time the pianist looked up from the keyboard, the woman had disappeared. On another occasion a crew member spotted a woman walking down the hallway at a time when only staff members were allowed onboard. He even followed her around several corners and watched her disappear into a private room. But as soon as he hurled open the door, no one was there.

Both the musician and the crew member reported their findings to their superiors. And both times they later noticed a portrait of Mary Greene on the wall and insisted that was the woman they had seen on the ship.

More than once, guests in Cabin 109—Mary's former room—have heard knocking on the wall. Of course, the crew cannot find anything that would cause the noise. Others report that locked doors fly open without explanation, and items fall off shelves without any vibrations on the boat. Moreover, stewards have been summoned to deliver meals or other items to Cabin 109, only to find an empty or ice cold room.

Captain Mary's reputation as a friendly spirit has captured the imagination of television viewers as well. In recent years the Discovery Channel, the History Channel, and the Travel Channel have featured Captain Mary and the *Delta Queen* on television shows that investigate haunted places.

Retired *Delta Queen* Captain Mike Williams believes the spirit of Captain Mary that still dwells on the boat is gentle and kind, always wanting the best for the *Queen* and its crew. And he is convinced that Captain Mary led him to his future wife.

Myra Frugé, a new employee on the *Delta Queen* in the mid-1980s, had no knowledge of the history of the riverboat or its protective spirit. But after rushing to check on a sick passenger in Cabin 109, she was stunned to find the room was empty. When she reported the mysterious incident to Captain Williams, he led her to the portrait of Mary Greene and told her about the presence of her spirit on the boat.

Less than one year later, Captain Williams and his new employee were married. Both credit the spirit of Captain Mary Greene for bringing them together. And both insist her spirit continues to live on the riverboat that is permanently docked in Chattanooga, making sure that all remains well and good on the magnificent *Delta Queen*.

CHAPTER 12

The Haunted Read House

The stately Sheraton Read House Hotel sits at the corner of Broad Street and Martin Luther King Jr. Boulevard in the heart of downtown Chattanooga, Tennessee. Every day tourists, residents, and businesspeople briskly walk past one of the city's most elegant landmarks. But few people realize that shadows of the past are still lurking behind the brick and terra-cotta facade of the ten-story hotel.

On the same parcel of land now occupied by the Read House, Thomas Crutchfield Sr. opened Chattanooga's first major hotel around 1847. According to some accounts, Crutchfield promised to build a grand hotel for train passengers if the owner of the Western and Atlantic Railroad would agree to make Chattanooga a major stop on the rails. When the first train traveled straight from Atlanta to Chattanooga on the Western and Atlantic rail lines on May 9, 1850, Crutchfield's hotel was open and ready to accommodate guests.

Crutchfield had wisely selected an ideal location for his hotel, directly across from the railroad depot. But crossing the street was no easy task for the first train passengers arriving in Chattanooga. The road was so muddy that the passengers had to walk on raised planks to get to the hotel. Despite the inconvenience, however, the large, three-story brick inn immediately prospered and became the social, economic, and political center of the town.

Shortly after the death of Crutchfield, his son Tom Jr. took over the hostelry. He quickly developed an excellent reputation as a businessman and innkeeper, and the popular Crutchfield son was soon elected mayor of Chattanooga.

A writer for *Harper's New Monthly Magazine* visited the city in 1857 and described the bustling activity at the Crutchfield House. It was "swarmed with people arriving and departing . . . hurrying to and fro with eager and excited looks, as if lives, fortunes, and sacred honor hung upon the events of the next hour. All the corners and byplaces were filled with groups in earnest conversation, some were handling bundles or papers, others examining maps."

Advertised as the "Regular House for passengers on trains to take meals," the Crutchfield House prospered throughout the 1850s. But as whispers of war swept through the nation and several southern states seceded from the Union, an ominous atmosphere engulfed Chattanooga.

One of the first signs of unrest in the city occurred in early 1861 when Jefferson Davis and his wife arrived in Chattanooga and spent the night at the Crutchfield House. Davis, who had just resigned from his seat in the US Senate, was returning home to Mississippi from Washington, D.C.

Word quickly spread of Davis's arrival, and a crowd gathered at the hotel, hoping to catch a glimpse of the senator and his wife, Varina. Seeing the growing crowd, a pair of local attorneys urged Davis to address the group of admirers. Though weary from his long journey, Davis spoke a few words and turned to leave the room. No sooner had he disappeared from sight than a melee erupted.

As soon as Davis left the room, William Crutchfield, Tom's brother, leaped up onto a counter and used it as a makeshift podium. He loudly declared that Davis was a traitor and condemned the man's claim that states had the right to secede. William Crutchfield, who had served on the local board of aldermen, was well known throughout the city as a devout Union loyalist with staunch beliefs that could not be swayed.

Spectators and participants later recounted several different versions of the chaotic situation that followed. According to one account, Crutchfield's tirade came to an abrupt halt because "the fury of the men forced him to quit speaking." Another report revealed that some men in the crowd pulled out their pistols. Tom Crutchfield, apparently fearing for his brother's life, yanked William down from the counter and rushed him out the back door.

The screams of some of the women present, including Varina Davis and one of the Crutchfield wives, only made matters worse, one account revealed. Much later Varina Davis blamed the entire confrontation on "the vagary of a drunken man."

Hearing of the confrontation, Davis went back to the room and discovered the furious crowd. According to one bystander, Davis said he was personally insulted by the situation. He also inquired about the person responsible for igniting the fury of the assembled group. Was his foe "responsible and reputable?" Was he up to the challenge of a duel?

Apparently, the conflict between Jefferson Davis and William Crutchfield ended that night in the Crutchfield House. No duel took place, and the Davis party departed peacefully the next day. But the confrontation at the Chattanooga hotel gained widespread attention across the southern states, and the town soon became known as a Union stronghold.

By April 1861 eight southern states had seceded from the Union, and volunteers throughout the South were using the railroads to reach the front line in Virginia. When the volunteer troops arrived at the train depot in Chattanooga, they immediately headed across the street to the Crutchfield House. Since the Confederacy had not arranged to feed any of the troops in transit, the hungry troops demanded meals.

Though Tennessee had not yet joined the Confederacy, Tom Crutchfield had little choice but to serve meals to the soldiers. Crutchfield later recalled one incident when an Arkansas regiment "loaded guns and fixed bayonets and marched in front of the house to mob me, calling me out and telling me they had been told that I was a Lincolnite and had said that I would not feed Jeff Davis or any of his Troops and gave me five minutes to explain."

By the time Tennessee joined the Confederacy in June 1861—the last of the eleven southern states to secede from the Union—Crutchfield was weary of contending with the soldiers' demands. Feeding the troops had personally cost him more than ten thousand dollars. Moreover, he was beginning to fear for the safety of his family—specifically, his mother, wife, and daughter—who resided with him at the Crutchfield House.

Crutchfield soon sold the hostelry and moved his family to a quieter setting outside of town. By 1863 the Civil War had engulfed Chattanooga, and Crutchfield's decision to sell his business proved to be a wise transaction. Union forces seized the hotel as its headquarters and converted the building into a hospital. According to one account, some five hundred soldiers received treatment at the site, and dozens of men died from their wounds at the Crutchfield House.

Though bullet holes scarred the structure, the Crutchfield House survived the ravages of war. The building even escaped ruin from the record flood of March 1867, although five feet of floodwaters penetrated the hotel. But the hostelry could not withstand the effects of the fire that engulfed and destroyed it later that year, burning the historic hotel to the ground.

Throughout the 1860s the Civil War stunted any growth of commerce in Chattanooga. By 1871, however, business was

The Sheraton Read House, 2012, stands on the same plot of land once occupied by the Crutchfield House in 1862.

slowly recovering. Seeing the need for a new place for visitors to stay in the center of town, Dr. John T. Read and his son, Samuel, opened a three-story hotel on the former site of the Crutchfield House. The hotel opened for business on New Year's Day in 1872 under the name Read House.

In 1879 son Samuel Read assumed management of the Read House, and the hotel earned a sterling reputation among travelers. To accommodate an increasing number of guests, the Reads added a fourth floor and expanded the capacity of the hotel to two hundred rooms in 1886. By the end of the nineteenth century, the magnificent Read House became one of the first commercial establishments in the city to boast electric lights.

In 1926 all but the north section of the hotel was demolished and replaced by the ten-story Georgian-style building with 414 rooms that remains today. Designed by Holabird and Roche, the new structure includes a mezzanine level overlooking a lobby with soaring columns, terrazzo floors inlaid with marble, and black walnut paneling. Most of the elaborate features, such as carved and gilded woodwork, mirrors recessed in massive arches, and Waterford chandeliers glittering from the twenty-five-foot ceiling of the Silver Ballroom, would be far too costly to be replicated today.

Though the establishment changed ownership several times after Samuel Read's death in 1942, the celebrated hotel continued to honor its past. Various owners maintained the architectural features of the landmark hotel. In 1977 the Read House was named to the National Register of Historic Places as a prime example of period architecture and decorative art.

The Read House also became the hotel of choice in Chattanooga for visiting dignitaries throughout the twentieth century. The hotel's guest list ranged from movie stars Tallulah Bankhead and Gary Cooper to statesmen and politicians such as Sir Winston Churchill and President Ronald Reagan. Even the notorious Al Capone was a hotel guest at one time.

In 2004 the hotel joined Starwood Hotels and Resorts as a member of the Sheraton family. The following year the Sheraton

Read House Hotel received an extensive renovation at a cost of ten million dollars, bringing the old hotel into the twenty-first century with modern touches such as Internet access and a new swimming pool.

Despite the elegance of the old hotel and the addition of modern amenities, an unexplainable presence has haunted the Read House since it opened in the 1920s. With the site's illustrious history, many theories about the ghostly spirits roaming through the old hotel revolve around the Civil War. Could ghosts of the soldiers who died at the old Crutchfield House still haunt the current hotel?

Undoubtedly, the agonizing deaths of dozens of soldiers occurred on the same plot of soil where the Sheraton Read House now stands. Murders and suicides that transpired at the old hotel are also blamed for the mysterious incidents that have defied explanation. One story tells of a lady of the night who was killed by a Yankee soldier at the hotel. Is the restless spirit of the murdered prostitute still making her presence known in the Chattanooga hotel?

Most of the staff members and guests who are familiar with the hotel's past believe the ghost of a former guest, Annalisa Netherly, occasionally makes an appearance at the Read House. According to local lore, Annalisa arrived in Chattanooga from San Francisco for an extended stay during the 1920s. Some say her husband accompanied her on the journey, while others contend that she was a prostitute.

Though no one is exactly certain of Annalisa's marital status, local legend maintains she experienced a horrific death in room 311 of the Read House. Some say she was bathing in the tub when her head was nearly severed. Whether she committed suicide or was murdered at the hands of a jealous lover or her own husband, no one knows for certain.

But staff and guests who have experienced the presence of Annalisa believe that her distraught presence still occupies room 311. Far too many times, guests staying in the room have heard knocking at the door. When they open the door, no one is there. Guests also have reported mirrors falling off the wall, the television cutting off with no warning, the sound of running water, and lights that turn off on their own. One television crew even discovered that their cameras failed to work in room 311. Was Annalisa responsible?

More than one guest has also claimed that the ghostly presence in room 311 is particularly angered by smoke, often putting out cigarettes. Out of respect for the ghost, the hotel staff did not allow smoking on the third floor, even during the era when smoking was permitted inside the hotel.

The hotel normally books room 311 only by request. If the hotel is full, however, guests who do not object or are not aware of the mysterious presence often check in to the room. More than once those guests have returned to the front desk in the middle of the night to request another room. Most of the time the guests say they can't explain their feelings, but they are far too uneasy to sleep in their assigned third-floor room.

One longtime hotel employee refused to believe in Annalisa's presence for the first thirty years that he worked at the Read

House. But he too became a believer after he encountered a confused young woman wearing an evening gown at the entrance to room 311. Leaving the door open, he left to fetch the hotel engineer to assist her. By the time they returned to the room, the woman had disappeared. Moreover, the door was sealed shut and locked from the inside—and the key failed to work.

Apparently, Annalisa's spirit is not limited to room 311. One day a small boy darted out of the mezzanine restroom and told his father that a woman wearing a long dress and with her hair pulled up from her neck was inside. The father immediately went into the room to investigate, but no one was there.

Another group of guests claimed to see Annalisa roaming the third floor. Many guests have reported strange entities on other floors of the hotel as well. Paranormal investigators believe supernatural energies are present in the halls and rooms, as well as the basement, which served as the morgue for the hospital that operated on the site during the Civil War.

Does the age of the building account for flickering lights, nonworking showers, dark shadows, and ghostly forms? Or are restless spirits of soldiers and jilted lovers roaming through the halls and consistently haunting room 311? Perhaps the history of the Read House and its predecessor, the Crutchfield House, are still keeping secrets behind the walls of the illustrious old hotel in Chattanooga, Tennessee.

CHAPTER 13

Meriwether Lewis's Mysterious Death

On October 10, 1809, Captain Meriwether Lewis stopped at a remote inn in Tennessee to spend the night as he traveled along the Natchez Trace. By daybreak the famed explorer was dying of gunshot wounds to the head and chest. He was only thirty-five years old.

No one knows exactly what transpired at Grinder's Stand, a log cabin with overnight lodging for travelers on the Natchez Trace, a pioneer trail that led through Tennessee. Many historians agree that Lewis committed suicide, while others contend he was murdered. For more than two hundred years, the intrigue surrounding the famous explorer's untimely death has become one of the enduring mysteries of Tennessee history.

Three years before Lewis's death, he and William Clark had finished the United States' first official expedition to the West Coast. The two men had crossed nearly eight thousand miles of wilderness from St. Louis to the Pacific Ocean and back. Following a hero's return, Lewis was appointed governor of the

Louisiana Territory. But by 1809 he was wrestling with allegations he had misused government funds. Determined to resolve the matter, Lewis packed his bags to head for Washington, D.C.

Lewis embarked on his journey on September 4, 1809, accompanied by his free servant, John Pernier, a former employee of Thomas Jefferson. The pair left St. Louis by boat, intending to float down the Mississippi to New Orleans and sail to the East Coast.

According to reports from witnesses, Lewis displayed bizarre behavior during the river journey, often drinking excessively. Lewis tried to commit suicide on two occasions, once by attempting to jump overboard and again by trying to shoot himself. He also made references in his journal to having "bilious fever" and taking "pills of opium and tartar." During a stop at Fort Pickering, located at the present site of Memphis, the fort commander held Lewis on twenty-four-hour suicide watch for more than a week.

Lewis recovered within a few days. At that point he decided to make the remainder of his journey by land. Major James Neely, a government agent for the Chickasaw Indians, agreed to accompany him. Armed with two pistols, a dagger, and a tomahawk, Lewis set off with Neely and their servants, along with several Chickasaw Indians.

On October 10, the morning after crossing the Tennessee River, Neely discovered two of his horses had strayed from their campsite during the night. Promising to meet Lewis at the next

Meriwether Lewis

inn along the Natchez Trace, Neelly stayed behind to look for the stray horses. Lewis continued on his way, riding alone along the rugged trail. Two servants trailed behind him, burdened by heavy trunks.

Later, Lewis stopped at Grinder's Stand, a remote inn seventy miles south of Nashville. According to some accounts, Lewis arrived at the inn with servants. By other accounts, he arrived alone.

According to the innkeeper, Mrs. Grinder, Lewis ate little supper, appeared angry, paced his room for several hours, and talked aloud to himself. At three o'clock in the morning, the sound of a gunshot awakened Mrs. Grinder. Then she heard a heavy thud, followed by the words "Oh, Lord!" and another pistol shot. Several minutes later Lewis called, "Oh, madam! Give me some water and heal my wounds."

Too frightened to move, Mrs. Grinder crouched fearfully in her room. At dawn she and the servants entered Lewis's room. Alive on the bed, Lewis revealed his bullet wounds to the group and offered money to anyone who would put him out of his misery. A few hours later he died.

By the time Major Neelly arrived at Grinder's Stand, Meriwether Lewis was dead. Neelly buried his friend nearby. In some versions of the story, Seaman, Lewis's loyal Newfoundland, who guarded his master against bears on the long journey west, remained by his grave, refusing to eat or drink. In other accounts the dog was never present at all.

Pernier headed on to Virginia and delivered the news of Lewis's suicide to Thomas Jefferson. No one claimed to have witnessed the shooting, and Pernier reported that the governor had killed himself. Lewis's close friends and acquaintances in the nation's capital accepted the servant's story.

Months later Jefferson wrote a short biography of Lewis and noted the explorer's depressive state. "While he lived with me in Washington, I observed at times sensible depressions of mind," Jefferson wrote. "During his western expedition the constant exertion which that required of all the faculties of body & mind, suspended these distressing affection; but after his establishment in St. Louis in sedentary occupations they returned upon him with redoubled vigor, and began seriously to alarm his friends. He was in a paroxysm of one of these when his affairs rendered it necessary for him to go to Washington."

Neelly later confided to Thomas Jefferson that Lewis "appeared at times deranged in mind" throughout the trip. Clark had also observed his companion's melancholy state. "I fear the weight of his mind has overcome him," he wrote after receiving word of Lewis's fate.

A year and a half after the shooting, ornithologist Alexander Wilson, one of Lewis's friends, became one of the first among many people to investigate the case. During a visit to Grinder's Stand, he interviewed Mrs. Grinder. Wilson documented the details about Lewis's death that he learned from Mrs. Grinder, who was the sole source of information about the last hours of Meriwether Lewis's life. Today, much of what historians know about the circumstances of his death has been gleaned from Wilson's interview with the innkeeper.

Several writers and scholars took firm stands that Lewis took his own life due to depression and alcoholism, along with personal and financial problems. Some believed he may have even planned the suicidal act before he left St. Louis. Shortly before embarking on his journey, Lewis had given several associates the power to distribute his possessions in the event of his death. He also composed his last will and testament while traveling down the Mississippi River.

One historian points out that Lewis, who never finished his expedition journals, may have felt like a failure. Though Lewis and Clark had journeyed over thousands of miles of wilderness with few casualties, they failed in the mission's primary goal of finding the Northwest Passage to the Pacific. Moreover, a system of trading posts that they'd established began to fall apart before the explorers returned home. And after spending most of his adult life as an adventurer and explorer, Lewis suddenly found himself in a sedentary desk job as governor of the Upper Louisiana Territory.

Others attribute Lewis's strange behavior and eventual self-destruction to debilitating diseases that deteriorated both his mind and body. Reimert T. Ravenholt, physician and epidemiologist, believes Lewis's bizarre behavior stemmed from paresis, a condition that causes impaired mental function due to brain damage from untreated syphilis. After studying the expedition diaries of both Lewis and Clark, Ravenholt concludes that Lewis probably contracted syphilis, a venereal disease, while on the western expedition.

In the secondary stage of syphilis about a month after exposure and infection, rashes on the skin typically occur. Lewis's expedition diary revealed that approximately four weeks after a night of dancing and partying with the Shoshoni tribe, "several of the men are unwell with the dysentery. Brakings out, or irruptions of the skin have also been common with us for some time."

Mental impairment occurs during the last stages of untreated syphilis, and Ravenholt noted that Lewis displayed such behavior shortly before he died. Rather than embarrass his friends and loved ones by admitting that he had contracted such an unmentionable disease, Lewis may have ended his own life.

Thomas C. Danisi, another Lewis and Clark scholar, believes Lewis was afflicted with malaria, which was known to cause bouts of dementia. Since malaria is spread by mosquitoes, the disease was not uncommon in the hot, humid climate of the South during the early nineteenth century. And once a person caught malaria, the disease could periodically reappear. The legendary David Crockett, for example, was known to suffer from several bouts of malaria during his lifetime.

One symptom of malaria is high fever, and Lewis's journal entries during his riverboat journey referred to "bilious fever." The "pills of opium and tartar," also referenced in Lewis's journal, could have been used to treat the malaria.

Some people were affected more strongly by malaria symptoms than others, and Danisi cites historical accounts and clinical studies of malaria patients who displayed bizarre behavior similar to that of Lewis during his final days. In severe cases patients have been known to inflict harm on the parts of the body that are filled with pain. Trying to kill the pain, however, they sometimes kill themselves. Could this have been the case with Lewis?

Though the people closest to Lewis believed he had substantial reasons for taking his own life, others were convinced he must have been murdered. Rumors about murder were circulating as soon as Lewis's death was made known. According to family lore, Lewis's mother believed he was murdered. After questioning Lewis's servant in the privacy of her own home in Virginia, she suspected that the servant had murdered her son. Other historical accounts contend that Lewis's mother had been well aware of her son's depressive state and accepted the fact that he had committed suicide.

In 1848 a commission of Tennesseans honored Lewis by erecting a marker over his grave. While examining the remains, committee members wrote that "it was more probable that he died at the hands of an assassin." Unfortunately, the report does not document the reasons for the committee's statement.

One historian and author contends that Lewis had far too many reasons to live to take his own life. After all, the Lewis and Clark expedition had catapulted Lewis into celebrity status as one of the first American heroes. Songs and poems were written about him, and he had been appointed governor of a large territory.

Some historians question why Lewis needed more than one bullet to kill himself. How could an expert marksman botch his own suicide and be forced to shoot himself twice? The logical assumption is that a much less-skilled marksman aimed the deadly bullets at Lewis. On the frontier trail travelers were easy prey for robberies and murders, considering the unlikely presence of eyewitnesses in the isolated setting of the Natchez Trace. For most proponents of the murder theory, the most plausible explanation is that unknown bandits killed Governor Lewis while robbing him.

The robbery-and-murder theory has led to a long list of possible suspects over the years, including many people who were near Lewis at the time of his death. Moreover, a combination of fact and fiction has given way to regional folklore. One of the most popular versions of the story is that Mr. Grinder, who was reportedly absent during the incident, returned home to find his wife in bed with Lewis. Enraged, he killed the famed explorer. As the story goes, Grinder was tried for murder and acquitted because everyone was afraid of him. No documents of the alleged trial, however, have ever been discovered.

Scholars have reconstructed lunar cycles to prove that the innkeeper's wife couldn't have seen what she said she saw that moonless night. Other accused murderers include John Pernier, Lewis's servant; Major Neelly; a local renegade named Runion; and even the Chickasaw chiefs who reportedly had been traveling with Lewis and Neelly.

Another theory for the robbery-and-murder motive focuses on a rumor that Lewis had discovered a gold mine during his western expedition. Upon his return he allegedly told friends about the mine and claimed to have drawn a map of its location. One journalist and historian contends that whether or not the rumor was true, many people may have believed Lewis may have been carrying the map with him at the time of his journey over the Natchez

Trace. His own servant, Major Neelly, the Chickasaw Indians in his party, or even bandits in the wilderness may have thought that robbing the governor of the map would lead to fortunes of gold.

Yet another theory surfaced in 1994 with the publication of *The Jefferson Conspiracies: A President's Role in the Assassination of Meriwether Lewis* by David Leon Chandler. The author contends Lewis was the victim of an assassination conspiracy set in motion by Thomas Jefferson. According to Chandler, Lewis had discovered secrets about General James Wilkinson, his predecessor as governor of Upper Louisiana. If the secrets were revealed, they would prove the general's guilt as a traitor—which would destroy the reputations of both Wilkinson and Jefferson. The real reason for Lewis's trip to Washington was to reveal the secrets, and the only way to kill the scandal was to kill Lewis before he could talk. Those traveling with Lewis in his final days, including Major Neelly, were also part of the conspiracy.

Today, Lewis's body rests beneath a twenty-foot-high stone monument at a milepost of the Natchez Trace Parkway, located in Meriwether Lewis Park at the site of the frontier inn where he died. A broken column symbolizes a life cut short at age thirty-five. The park is situated in Lewis County, named in honor of the explorer and statesman, near Hohenwald, Tennessee.

In 1993 about two hundred of Lewis's descendants, along with a team of forensic scientists, launched a campaign to exhume his body. Since Lewis never married or had children, the descendents are related to his sister, Jane. Family members believe DNA samples from several female descendents could permit scientists to confirm that the remains belong to Lewis. After all, corpses were not uncommon along the Natchez Trace. At the very least they could discover his height or the color of his hair—two distinguishing features that have been lost in history.

Moreover, exhuming the body means they could possibly learn about Lewis's health or discover if he had suffered from syphilis or malaria. Forensic scientists could also analyze the skull to see if he had been shot at close range—or at the hands of another. If the bullet entered the back of his skull, for example, suicide would have been unlikely.

In 1996 a coroner's jury in Tennessee recommended Lewis be exhumed to collect evidence. But a federal court ruled in 1998 that the National Park Service had the last word. Policies of the National Park Service prohibit exhumations unless burial sites are "threatened with destruction by park development, operational activities or natural forces." Officials say that digging up Lewis could intrude upon the nearby burial sites of more than one hundred pioneers. Moreover, Lewis's body lies under a foot and a half of concrete and at least three feet of crushed gravel, which would make exhumation both difficult and costly.

Lewis's descendants cited other exhumations on land belonging to the National Park Service, including one in a cemetery at another section of the Natchez Trace Parkway. Impressed by the family's overwhelming quest to uncover the truth, a federal government official expressed written support for exhumation in

2008. The official stated that an exhumation was "appropriate and in the public interest," given "the unique circumstances of the death of Meriwether Lewis."

But before preparations for the exhumation were complete, the agency reversed its decision, arguing that department policy couldn't be ignored. Citing more than three million dollars in federal allocations to improve the site, the US Department of the Interior instructed the family to consider the National Park Service's refusal to dig up the body as "a final decision on this matter."

Are answers to the mystery of Meriwether Lewis's death buried beneath the monument? Would an exhumation shed light on the mystery? And would a forensic examination change anyone's mind about the true circumstances of Lewis's death?

Next to Lewis's gravesite a plaque states that his life drew "mysteriously to its close" at this place in 1809, three years after his epic journey to the Pacific Ocean. Today, more than two hundred years after his death, the mystery remains unsolved.

CHAPTER 14

The Mistress of Belmont Mansion

At the heart of Belmont University in Nashville is a magnificent mansion that was once the home of a wealthy Southern belle by the name of Adelicia Acklen. With a reputation for being high-spirited and manipulative, Adelicia was the driving force behind the construction of her beloved Belmont estate before the Civil War. And more than 160 years later, some suspect the intriguing Adelicia has never left the premises.

When Adelicia was born on March 15, 1817, she became the youngest member of a family that had already made a mark on the city of Nashville, Tennessee. Her father, Oliver Bliss Hayes, was a prominent Nashville lawyer and judge, as well as a Presbyterian minister and land speculator. He also shared the same last name as President Rutherford B. Hayes, who happened to be his cousin.

At the age of twenty-two, Adelicia married Isaac Franklin of Sumner County, Tennessee. A fifty-year-old businessman and plantation owner, Isaac was a wealthy cotton planter and slave trader. Together, they had four children.

While visiting one of his Louisiana plantations in 1846, Isaac died unexpectedly from a stomach virus. Widowed after only seven years of marriage, Adelicia inherited her late husband's estate. Valued at an estimated one million dollars, the estate included seven Louisiana cotton plantations with nearly nine thousand acres of land; Fairvue, a two-thousand-acre farm in Middle Tennessee; more than fifty thousand acres of undeveloped land in Texas; stocks and bonds; and 750 slaves.

Though independently wealthy before age thirty, Adelicia suffered much loss during her early adult years. Along with the death of her husband, she experienced the loss of her entire family. None of the couple's four children survived beyond the age of eleven. Most likely, the children were victims of the high rate of infant mortality during the nineteenth century.

Romance, however, soon blossomed once again in Adelicia's life. At her home in downtown Nashville, Adelicia married Colonel Joseph Alexander Smith Acklen, a hero of the Mexican War, on May 8, 1849. Earlier in the year, Adelicia had purchased three parcels of land in Nashville, apparently for the purpose of constructing a new home after her marriage to Joseph. Independent Adelicia must have insisted on retaining control of the wealth that she had accumulated before the wedding. Her new husband, a lawyer from Huntsville, Alabama, signed a prenuptial contract that gave her complete control over all of her businesses, property, and assets.

Immediately after the wedding, the couple began construction on an elaborate estate named Belle Monte, meaning "beautiful mountain" in Italian, on the 180 acres of land that Adelicia had recently purchased. Built in the style of an Italian villa, the family home was surrounded by elaborate circular gardens, fountains, an artificial lake, and a greenhouse and conservatory that stretched two hundred feet in length.

No expense was spared in designing and building the lavish estate. A water tower provided a source for irrigating the gardens and supplying water for the fountains. The estate even operated its own refinery, which provided gas for lighting. The grounds held a bear house, a deer park, and even a zoo. Since public zoos did not exist at the time, Adelicia eventually opened the estate to Nashville citizens, allowing the public to enjoy the wild animals in her private zoo.

After four years of construction, the Acklens and their new son, Joseph, moved into their luxurious home. Located two miles from downtown Nashville, the house was even more spectacular than the grounds. Adelicia lavishly furnished the mansion for entertainment, including a bowling alley with a billiards parlor, and an art gallery. Fine furniture, paintings, and marble statues filled every room of the home. Venetian glass adorned the windows, doors, and transoms. A ten-foot-wide octagonal cupola crowned the top of the house, venting the rooms during the heat of the summer and providing an "astronomical observatory" for viewing the estate and downtown Nashville.

Around 1857 the Acklens added east and west wings to the main structure. The exterior was lathed in stucco, scored to

This image, taken by photographer Lester Jones on August 19, 1940, was part of a Historic American Buildings Survey. This view is of Belmont's south elevation.

resemble cut stone, and painted pink. The same shade of pink remains on the house today.

Two years later, the Acklens hired Adolphus Heiman, a Prussian architect working in Nashville, to enlarge and remodel Belmont Mansion. Heiman enclosed the back porch to create the fifty-eight-foot-long Grand Salon, described by architectural historians as "the most elaborate domestic space built in antebellum Tennessee." The magnificent room featured a barrel-vaulted ceiling soaring twenty-two feet in height, ornate plaster cornices, a freestanding staircase, and Corinthian columns.

With this new addition, Belmont Mansion contained thirty-six rooms and approximately ten thousand square feet of living space. The family living quarters consisted of ten bedrooms, two dining rooms, a library, an impressive front hall, and a host of family and entertaining parlors. An additional 8,400 square feet in the basement held the kitchen and other service areas. Always the consummate hostess, Adelicia hosted some of Nashville's most elaborate parties at Belmont Mansion. Famous for her balls and parties at Belmont estate, Adelicia welcomed such notable guests as President Andrew Johnson, Alexander Graham Bell, and Thomas Huxley.

Joseph's superb skills as a businessman and plantation manager paid off handsomely. By 1860 he had tripled his wife's fortune. With their wealth, the Acklens lived a luxurious lifestyle. During the summer, they lived at Belmont. During the winter, they traveled to Louisiana and lived on their plantations. Along the way they became the parents of six children. Unfortunately, two of the children died during childhood.

When the winds of war began to sweep through the South in the early 1860s, Adelicia and her children chose to stay in Nashville throughout the year, opting not to travel to Louisiana each winter. But while tending to one of Adelicia's Louisiana plantations, Joseph died on September 11, 1863.

At the time of Joseph's death, 2,800 bales of cotton belonging to the Acklens had been placed in storage in Louisiana. When the Confederate army threatened to burn the cotton to keep it from falling into Union possession, Adelicia refused to idly stand by in Tennessee and lose the fortune to theft or destruction.

Adelicia boldly set off for Louisiana, accompanied only by a female cousin. Determined not to face financial ruin, she secretly negotiated with both the Confederate and Union armies to save her fortune. After securing promises from the Confederates not to burn her cotton, she convinced the Union army to help her move the bales to New Orleans, which was under Union control. At one point she even convinced Confederate forces to serve as escorts for a Yankee wagon train filled with her cotton as it pressed forward to New Orleans.

Once the bales had arrived safely in New Orleans, they were loaded on a ship bound for England. Though fully aware that selling the cotton to a broker in England was illegal according to military law, Adelicia shrewdly brokered a deal with the Rothschilds of London, exchanging the cotton for a reported $960,000 in gold. Less than a month after Confederate Robert E. Lee surrendered to Union forces, Adelicia and her children rushed to Europe to collect the money from the sale of the cotton.

During the first two weeks of December 1864, Union General Thomas J. Wood occupied Belmont Mansion before the battle of Nashville. Though the lavish gardens were damaged as thirteen thousand Union soldiers camped on the grounds during the occupation, the mansion and its lavish contents remained unscathed during the Civil War.

In 1867 Dr. William Cheatham, a respected Nashville physician, became the third husband of Adelicia Hayes Franklin Acklen. Like her second husband, William also signed a prenuptial agreement. About two thousand wedding guests attended the wedding reception at Belmont.

For nearly twenty years, the couple spent the majority of their time at Belmont in Nashville. Shortly before Christmas 1884, however, Adelicia left her husband and traveled with three of her children to Orlando, Florida, for the winter. Few realized she was leaving not only her husband but her magnificent Belmont Mansion on a permanent basis.

Though the exact cause of Adelicia's separation from her third husband is not clear, some records indicate that William resided in a local boardinghouse after Adelicia asked him to leave the mansion. Other records reveal Adelicia and her children returned to Nashville and lived in a rented house for a short time after spending the winter in Florida. At one point Adelicia's oldest son, Joseph, a bachelor, lived at Belmont.

Adelicia and three of her adult children permanently moved to Washington, D.C., in 1886. The following year she sold Belmont to a land development company that proposed to develop the estate into a subdivision. A few months later Adelicia contracted pneumonia during a shopping trip to New York City and died in a Fifth Avenue hotel on May 4, 1887. Her body was returned to Nashville and buried in the family mausoleum at Mount Olivet Cemetery alongside her first two husbands and, eventually, nine of her ten children.

In 1889 two women from Philadelphia, Miss Hereon and Miss Hood, purchased Belmont Mansion and thirteen acres of the estate. Within a year the women had opened up the mansion as a school for girls. The bedrooms located on the second floor and most of the first-floor bedrooms were turned into dormitory rooms, as were the formal dining room and the billiards room. One of the parlors became the school library. Over the next decade several new buildings were added to the school to accommodate the growing number of students.

The school merged with Nashville's Ward Seminary in 1913 and became an academy and junior college for women under the name Ward-Belmont. The Tennessee Baptist Convention purchased the institution in 1951 and reopened the school as Belmont College, a coeducational four-year liberal arts college. The mansion became the student center for the new school.

In 1972 Belmont Mansion was placed on the National Register of Historic Places. At the same time, a group of Nashville residents formed the Historic Belmont Association to preserve, restore, and maintain the historic site. Today this group is known as the Belmont Mansion Association.

Renovation of the mansion started as soon as the association was formed. The group immediately removed some of the dormitory walls and began renovation on two upstairs rooms. They also removed many items of furniture that did not date back to the nineteenth century and retained only period pieces. Some of the remaining items were original to the house.

By 1976 eight renovated rooms were opened to the public for tours. Diligent restoration efforts for nearly forty years have resulted in the opening of more rooms for touring, including the library, small study, family and formal dining rooms, and additional bedrooms.

Today, Belmont Mansion is the largest house museum in Tennessee and one of the few nineteenth-century homes with a history that centers on the life of a woman. It is also the second-largest pre–Civil War mansion in the South. Belmont University, a liberal arts school with more than six thousand undergraduate and graduate students, owns the mansion, while restoration and operation of the building is administered by the historical association.

The original water tower, stretching 105 feet into the air, remains on the grounds. Visitors can see traces of the ornamental gardens that once graced the lawn, as well as original gazebos, marble statutes, and the largest collection of nineteenth-century cast-iron garden ornaments in the United States.

Approximately half of the house is open to the public for guided tours. Victorian furnishings and decorative items reflect the opulent lifestyle of Adelicia and her family. The mansion displays an impressive collection of marble statutes and mantels, oil paintings, and gilded mirrors that once belonged to the Acklens. Much of the original Venetian glass remains in the house. To protect windows from the sun, covered porches with cast-iron balconies surround the mansion.

Some claim the atmosphere within the partially restored Belmont Mansion resounds with the spirit of Adelicia, making it seem as though she has never left her beloved Belmont. Many Belmont students, visitors, and staff members have reported sensing her presence. After touring Adelicia's private quarters, for instance, some visitors have heard footsteps behind them as they descended the stairs. Glancing to the rear, the guests could see nothing on the staircase. Each time they stopped their descent, the footsteps suddenly ceased. And once the visitors resumed walking, the mysterious sound of footsteps resumed.

During the Christmas season the university often holds special events at Belmont Mansion. Although the festivities may not be as extravagant as the holiday celebrations hosted by Adelicia, the former owner has frequently made her presence known during these Christmas parties. Students preparing for the holidays have heard footsteps that seem to come from Adelicia's private quarters, sounding much like the sound of a woman's footsteps pacing the room.

University employees and construction workers also claim they have experienced mysterious events in the house, and they attribute the strange occurrences to Adelicia's ghostly presence. While laborers attempted to renovate Adelicia's bedroom, a wall collapsed abruptly and inexplicably. One worker's tools were lost in the chaos. On another occasion a Belmont employee stayed overnight in a room near the main hall of the house. But after hearing many unexplainable noises during the night, the woman became so frightened that she packed up and left the premises.

THE MISTRESS OF BELMONT MANSION

Portraits of several of the Acklen children who died during childhood are displayed throughout the mansion. Numerous visitors have reported the strange sensation of being watched as they admired the paintings.

Still, some people may argue that old houses are often drafty, causing sudden chills that cannot be explained. Older structures are also known to creak and groan as they age. Or is it possible that the spirit of Adelicia is the cause of the mysterious sounds?

Eyewitnesses of a ghostly presence in the house are convinced that Adelicia still roams through the mansion. During the 1960s several students were studying for final examinations in one of the mansion's rooms that had been designated as a study lounge. As the students studied late into the night, a ghostly presence appeared before them, wearing an elegant white gown. The students also reported the woman had black hair and radiated with a special beauty, much like the portraits of Adelicia Acklen. Though stunned, the curious girls attempted to follow the ghostly spirit through the house. But the ghost soon disappeared into thin air.

According to one of the most famous Belmont legends, one of the mansion's mantel clocks stopped ticking at the moment of Joseph Acklen's death. Later, the clock operated perfectly as long as it remained on the mantel in Joseph's sitting room. Once it was removed from the mantel, the clock would stop again.

One of the most mystifying encounters occurred at the mansion when a photographer for the university yearbook attempted to snap a picture of the ticking clock after it had been placed on the mantel in Joseph's sitting room. Once the film was developed into prints, the photographer was stunned to discover the picture included the image of a lady wearing a hooded cloak. The photographer insisted no other person had been present in the room when he had taken the shot. Moreover, the photo—taken long before the days of digital photography—did not appear to have been altered in any way.

Photographs reportedly have also captured the mysterious ghost of Adelicia Acklen in front of a mirror inside the mansion. Security guards claim they have seen her ghostly form roaming through the mansion, appearing worried and dismayed. Some students say they have seen her presence on the grounds, as well as inside the house.

Some speculators contend Adelicia is searching through the house for her dead children. Others insist she is worried that her beloved mansion may be demolished to make room for new university buildings. No matter the reason, Adelicia Hayes Franklin Acklen Cheatham may still be present in the mansion she once called her beloved Belle Monte.

BIBLIOGRAPHY

THE BELL WITCH HAUNTING

Monahan, Brent. *The Bell Witch: An American Haunting.* New York: St. Martin Press, 1997.

"Tennessee Myths and Legends: Bell Witch." Tennessee State Library and Archives. tennessee.gov/tsla/exhibits/myth/bellwitch.htm. Accessed May 14, 2012.

THE SECRETS OF THE LOST SEA

Crutchfield, Jennifer. "The Legend and the Secrets of the Lost Sea." chattanoogaparentmagazine.com/2011/12/the-legend-and-the-secrets-of-the-lost-sea. Accessed May 13, 2012.

"The Lost Sea Adventure." thelostsea.com. Accessed May 22, 2012.

Wyatt, Jim. "Exploration of the Lost Sea." thedecostop.com. Accessed July 9, 2012.

THE WHITE MARBLE MAUSOLEUM WITH CRIMSON STAINS

Hooker, Timothy W. "The Red Streaks on the White Mausoleum." appalachianhistory.net/2010/10/the-red-streaks-on-the-white-mausoleum.html. Accessed June 8, 2012.

Manley, Roger. *Weird Tennessee.* New York: Sterling Publishing Co., 2010.

THE MYSTERY OF THE MELUNGEONS

Davis, Louise Littleton. *Frontier Tales of Tennessee.* Gretna, LA: Pelican Publishing Company, 1976.

Loller, Travis. "Racial Identity." Chattanooga, TN: *Chattanooga Times Free Press,* May 28, 2012, B3.

McGowan, Kathleen. "Where do we really come from?" *Discover Magazine,* May 2003.

Toplovich, Ann. "Melungeons." *Tennessee Encyclopedia of History and Culture.* Tennnessee Historical Society, tennesseeencyclopedia.net/entry.php?rec=888. Accessed June 25, 2012.

THE LEGEND OF DAVY CROCKETT

Crockett, David. *A Narrative of the Life of David Crockett of the State of Tennessee: A Facsimile Reproduction with Annotations and Introduction by James A. Shackford and Stanley F. Folmsbee.* Knoxville, TN: University of Tennessee Press, 1973.

Gronemann, William, III. *David Crockett: Hero of the Common Man.* New York: Forge Books, 2005.

Lofaro, Michael A. *Davy Crockett: The Man, the Legend, the Legacy, 1786–1986.* Knoxville, TN: University of Tennessee Press, 1986.

THE GHOST OF BRINKLEY FEMALE COLLEGE

"Brinkley Female College (Ghost House) Written Historical and Descriptive Data." Historic American Buildings Survey West Tennessee Project. National Park Service, Summer 1972. memory.loc.gov/pnp/habshaer/tn/tn0100/tn0127/data/tn0127data.pdf. Accessed September 2, 2012.

Brown, Alan. *Haunted Places in the American South.* Jackson, MS: University Press of Mississippi, 2002.

"Memphis' Most Famous Ghost Story," Tennessee State Library and Archives. tennessee.gov/tsla/exhibits/myth/ghosts.htm. Accessed September 4, 2012.

Robertson, J. R. *The Brinkley Female College Ghost Story.* Memphis, TN: R. C. Floyd & Co., 1871.

THE HAUNTED HALES BAR DAM

Archambault, Paul. "Hale's Bar Dam Powerhouse." National Register of Historic Places Registration Form, n.d. media.timesfreepress.com/docs/2008/09/Hales_Bar_Dam_Powerhouse.pdf. Accessed September 6, 2012.

Ghost Adventures: Hales Bar Marina and Dam. Travel Channel video. travelchannel.com/tv-shows/ghost-adventures/ episodes/hales-bar-marina-and-dam. Accessed September 2, 2012.

Livingood, James W. *A History of Hamilton County, Tennessee.* Memphis, TN: Memphis State University Press, 1981.

THE MUMMY MYSTERY

Bates, Finis L. *The Escape and Suicide of John Wilkes Booth: Or the First True Account of Lincoln's Assassination, Containing a Complete Confession by Booth Many Years After His Crime.* Memphis, TN: J. L. Nichols & Company, 1907.

Finger, Michael. "Mummy Mystery." *Memphis Flyer,* September 20, 2007. memphisflyer.com/memphis/mummy-mystery/ Content?oid=1139510. Accessed August 8, 2012.

Nilsson, Jeff. "The Assassin's Mummy; or, John Wilkes Booth's Second Career." *Saturday Evening Post,* April 14, 2012. saturdayeveningpost.com/2012/04/14/archives/then-and-now/the-assassins-mummy-john-wilkes-booths-post-mortem-career.html. Accessed August 9, 2012.

Portman, Jed. "Historical vertebrae, a sideshow mummy and the lingering mystery of John Wilkes Booth." PBS *Need to Know,* April 12, 2011. pbs.org/wnet/need-to-know/culture/ historical-vertebrae-a-sideshow-mummy-and-the-lingering-mystery-of-john-wilkes-booth/8560/. Accessed August 9, 2012.

CHEROKEE MYTHS AND LEGENDS

"Cherokee Myths and Legends." Tennessee State Library and Archives. tennessee.gov/tsla/exhibits/myth/index.htm and tennessee.gov/tsla/exhibits/myth/nativeamericans.htm. Accessed September 22, 2012.

Mooney, James. *Myths of the Cherokee.* Washington, DC: Government Printing Office, 1902.

THE MYSTERY OF THE OLD STONE FORT

Faulkner, Charles H. *The Old Stone Fort.* Knoxville, TN: University of Tennessee Press, 1971.

———. "Old Stone Fort State Archaeological Park." tennesseeencyclopedia.net/entry.php?rec=1018, February 23, 2011. Accessed September 1, 2012.

McMahan, Basil B. *The Mystery of the Old Stone Fort.* Nashville, TN: Tennessee Book Company, 1965.

THE *DELTA QUEEN*'S MARY GREENE

Kotarski, Georgianna C. *Ghosts of the Southern Tennessee Valley.* Winston-Salem, NC: John F. Blair Publisher, 2006.

Lyons, Ben. "*Delta Queen* Revisited." *Cruise Travel,* March/April 2012, vol. 33, issue 5, n.p.

Putnam, Yolanda. "Discovery Looking for *Delta Queen* Ghost." *Chattanooga Times Free Press.* September 24, 2009, n.p.

"The River People: Captain Mary Becker Greene." National Mississippi River Museum & Aquarium. mississippirivermuseum.com/features_halloffame_detail .cfm?memberID=11. Accessed September 1, 2012.

Scull, Theodore W. "Mary of *Delta Queen*." *Cruise Travel,* May/June 2007, vol. 28, issue 6, n.p.

THE HAUNTED READ HOUSE

"Hotel's History." The Sheraton Read House Hotel Chattanooga. sheratonreadhouse.com/history. Accessed September 8, 2012.

Kotarski, Georgianna C. *Ghosts of the Southern Tennessee Valley.* Winston-Salem, NC: John F. Blair Publisher, 2006.

Livingood, James W. *A History of Hamilton County, Tennessee.* Memphis, TN: Memphis State University Press, 1981.

MERIWETHER LEWIS'S MYSTERIOUS DEATH

Brown, Dee. "What Really Happened to Meriwether Lewis?" *Columbia Magazine.* Winter 1988, vol. 1, no. 4.

Esterl, Mike. "Meriwether Lewis's Final Journey Remains a Mystery." *The Wall Street Journal,* September 24, 2010. online .wsj.com/article/SB10001424052748703384204575509582 853734648.html. Accessed October 5, 2012.

Meriwether Lewis Park (Natchez Trace Parkway). National Park Service. www.nps.gov/history/history/online_books/ lewisandclark/site38.htm. Accessed October 20, 2012.

Ravenholt, Reimert Thorolf. "History Commentary—Self-Destruction on the Natchez Trace: Meriwether Lewis's Act of Ultimate Courage." *Columbia Magazine,* vol. 13 #2 (Summer 1999): 3–6. columbia.washingtonhistory.org/magazine/ articles/1999/0299/0299-a1.aspx. Accessed October 20, 2012.

"Theories and Interpretations of Meriwether Lewis' Death," Lewis & Clark in Columbia River Country. stories .washingtonhistory.org/LC-columbia/teaching/pdfs/Theories .pdf. Accessed October 5, 2012.

Tucker, Abigail. "Meriwether Lewis' Mysterious Death." Smithsonian.com, October 9, 2009. smithsonianmag.com/ history-archaeology/Meriwether-Lewis-Mysterious-Death. Accessed October 4, 2012.

The Mistress of Belmont Mansion

Barefoot, Daniel W. *Haunted Halls of Ivy: Ghosts of Southern Colleges and Universities.* Winston-Salem, NC: John F. Blair, 2004.

Belmont Mansion: "History." belmontmansion.com/mansionhistory/. Accessed October 3, 2012.

"Belmont Mansion, Nashville," Tennessee State Library and Archives. tennessee.gov/tsla/exhibits/myth/ghosts.htm. Accessed October 3, 2012.

Brown, Mark. "Adelicia Acklen (1817–1887)," *Tennessee Encyclopedia of History and Culture.* tennesseeencyclopedia.net/entry.php?rec=1. Accessed October 3, 2012.

———. "Belmont Mansion." *Tennessee Encyclopedia of History and Culture.* tennesseeencyclopedia.net/entry.php?rec=78. Accessed October 3, 2012.

INDEX

ABOUT THE AUTHOR

Susan Sawyer enjoys exploring the past and writing about historical topics. History serves as the centerpiece for many of her writings, taking form in both fact and fiction. Drawing upon her fascination with the history of her native South, Susan is the author of fifteen books, including Globe Pequot Press's *More Than Petticoats: Remarkable Tennessee Women* and *It Happened in Tennessee*.

A graduate of the University of Tennessee, Susan worked as a magazine editor and communications consultant before establishing a career as a freelance writer and published author. Today she writes from her home in Tennessee, where she lives with her husband, Ron.